TWO SQUARES

ISBN 0-935617-89-2
ISBN 978-0-93561-789-4

Book and cover design by Wilcox Design
Printed and bound by Maple-Vail Book Manufacturing Group

The Harvard University Graduate School of Design is a leading center for education, information, and technical expertise on the built environment. Its departments of Architecture, Landscape Architecture, and Urban Planning and Design offer masters and doctoral degree programs and provide the foundation for its Advanced Studies and Executive Education programs.

THE AGA KHAN PROGRAM AT THE
HARVARD UNIVERSITY GRADUATE SCHOOL OF DESIGN
CAMBRIDGE, MASSACHUSETTS

2 TWO SQUARES

MARTYRS SQUARE, BEIRUT, AND SIRKECI SQUARE, ISTANBUL

EDITED BY **HASHIM SARKIS** WITH MARK DWYER AND PARS KIBARER

DISTRIBUTED BY HARVARD UNIVERSITY PRESS

CONTENTS

Preface
HASHIM SARKIS 06

Acknowledgments 08

Part 1: Beirut   **Square One: Martyrs Square, Downtown Beirut**

A Vital Void:
Reconstructions of   Considering Public
Downtown Beirut   Reclaiming the Bourj   Life in Beirut
HASHIM SARKIS 10   SAMIR KHALAF 24   MARK DWYER 50

Square One Studio: Square One Studio:
Site and Context 58   Student Work 60

David Cutler   Reem Alissa
Claudia Mejia   David Fletcher
Hamad Al-Eisa   Anna-Maria Bulska
Shannon Bassett   Samuel Olbekson
Abby Feldman   Yutaka Sho
Aaron Cohen

Part 2: Istanbul

Intermodal Istanbul, Sirkeci Square

On the Regeneration
of the Golden Horn
TANSEL KORKMAZ 96

Sirkeci Square:
The Evolution of a Transient Space
PARS KIBARER 114

Intermodal Istanbul Studio:
Site and Context 128

Intermodal Istanbul
Studio: Student Work 130

Chris White
David Brown
Chung-Chien Chiang
Kensuke Soejima
Justine Kwiatkowski
Kotchakorn Voraakhom
Kristin Hopkins

Natalie Rinne
Oscar Oliver
Phoebe Schenker
Sarah Holton
Thomas Hussey
Ahmed Khadier

This publication documents the research, discussions, and projects generated by two studio classes held at the Harvard University Graduate School of Design in the spring semesters of 2004 and 2005. Both studios focused on the design of a major public space in an eastern Mediterranean city that is undergoing significant urban transformation. Both studios set out to test the potential that large open spaces hold for the revitalization of historic urban centers despite the decentralization that these two cities, Beirut and Istanbul, have undergone in the last twenty years. Such public spaces, however, will have to take on a very different countenance to maintain their historic vitality.

The fact that they are to regain their roles as major transportation hubs undoubtedly will generate new energy. Yet in both cases it was important to link this enhanced daily use with the encouragement of public activities. The charge of both studios was to develop this vitality without falling into the hyper-programming approach, the "theming" of activities and scripting of urban life. The explorations extended from the belief that the uses of public space should be open to both interpretation by their users and change over time, and that the role of the designer is to orchestrate the components of urban space to allow for these potentials to be played out.

Three main challenges confront such an undertaking. First, the idea of orchestrating the different components requires expanding the scope of the designer of the public space to include control of infrastructure, landscape, and urban "accessories"—in other words, all potential dimensions of urban life. Even though one person can rarely master all of the skills implied by such a widened scope, the studios sought to use design as a tool for the orchestration of different elements, if not their total control.

Second, the challenge of deferring the scripting of spaces to users could lead either to the creation of dauntingly large, empty spaces that ultimately diminish the scale and impact of

PREFACE any social activity or to the dismissal of design as a means by

which public space could be shaped. The projects in this publication, we hope, prove that the range of possibilities between those two extremes is wide.

Third, the nature of decision-making about public spaces in today's cities rarely allows for total control over complex intermodal and multifaceted public spaces. For example, decisions about the shaping of archeological sites rarely overlap with those about modes of transportation, and chaotic and fragmented public spaces such as Sirkeci or Martyrs Square often reflect the difficult and coordinated politics of urban planning even if this lack of coordination tends to produce their most characteristic and, one can dare say, essentially urban aspects. In other words, if an overall "master design" were possible, the challenge would be to orchestrate without compromising such urban qualities as the contingencies of accidental encounters, of functions spilling into each other, of purposeful crowds erupting out of seemingly disconnected individuals.

These, in brief, are the main challenges that confronted the two studios and against which the students set out to develop their propositions. Their projects were greatly influenced by their collective and individual research on the histories of these sites and similar conditions elsewhere, but they also greatly benefited from the input of scholars such as Professors Samir Khalaf and Tansel Korkmaz, whose deep social and historical knowledge of the squares in Beirut and Istanbul, respectively, is evidenced in the papers included in this publication. Through their words and the designs of the students, we hope that this publication contributes to a greater understanding of the history and design potentials of public space.

This is the first in a series of publications that the Aga Khan Program at the Harvard University Graduate School of Design is producing and distributing in cooperation with Harvard University Press. I would like to thank the Aga Khan Trust for Culture for its support of the program activities and for the special grant that supports the publication series. I would also like to thank Sara Davis at the Harvard University Press for her enthusiastic collaboration.

I am grateful to Melissa Vaughn, director of publications at the GSD, for guidance in launching the series; to book designer Jean Wilcox, for establishing the series identity with the design of this first volume; to Neyran Turan, publications coordinator of the Aga Khan Program, for seeing the project through to realization; and to Robin Brinckerhoff and Maria Moran for their administrative support.

For the Beirut section of the book, I am also grateful to the collaborators on this venture, namely Solidere's town-planning team, especially Angus Gavin, Amira Solh, and Fadi Jamali, and the Department of Architecture at the American University of Beirut. Professor Samir Khalaf's input, both in Beirut and in this publication, left a strong impression on the students. The studio also benefited from the participation of many visitors and critics during the semester, including Amale Andraos, Ilham Makdissi, Richard Sommer, Nader Tehrani, Charles Waldheim, and Dan Wood.

For the Istanbul project, I would like to thank the Municipality of Istanbul and Mayor Kadir Topbaş for their hospitality and for supplying us with the necessary data and information. I would also like to thank Bilgi University's School of Architecture for hosting us in Istanbul. The students also benefited from the feedback of Mustafa Abadan, Alparslan Ataman, Farès el-Dahdah, Dorothée Imbert, Richard Sommer, Han Tümertekin, Neyran Turan, Sarah Whiting, and Attila Yücel. I would also like to thank Chris White for his help in editing this section of the publication.

ACKNOWLEDGMENTS

1

Part 1: Beirut

Square One: Martyrs Square, Downtown Beirut

HASHIM SARKIS

A VITAL VOID:

Reconstructions of Downtown Beirut

> I looked this way and that way. I could not believe what I saw: level ground, empty, like an open palm of the hand, a horizontal expanse, leveled and paved over, its even surface unmarred by any stray objects or protrusions. . . The sea, I said. I must find the sea. . . If I cannot find the sea, then I am either dreaming or mad. I will walk down to the sea. From there, I will try to see where I am, pinpoint my location. And from there, I will figure out the direction the shop lies in, or I'll see some landmark, something to guide me, so I can reorient myself to go on.
>
> —Hoda Barakat, *The Tiller of Waters*

A few lines before the end of *The Tiller of Waters,* the novel's protagonist, Nicholas Mitri, wakes up to find himself in a void. He gradually realizes that this void is actually the center of Beirut, which he has inhabited alone during the 1975–90 civil war—and which he desperately tried to describe and thus preserve throughout the novel. Mitri, a Greek Orthodox from the predominantly Muslim West Beirut, was forced out of his house by Shiite Muslim refugees from South Lebanon who had themselves been displaced by an Israeli invasion. He drifted to his father's textile shop in downtown Beirut, the contested battle zone between Christian East and Muslim West Beirut. There he lived alone in the wilderness of the city center and recounted his family's story and the history of the different peoples and religious groups that inhabited his life and the prewar city.

The house where he lived with his Greek-Alexandrian parents and with the Kurdish maid he loved, the shop owned by a Sunni Muslim next to his father's in the bazaar of downtown Beirut, the parlor where his mother was trained by an Armenian piano teacher, are all eventually wiped out—not by the war but by the reconstruction project. The void, at the end of the story, represents the futility of Mitri's efforts to preserve these places. The buildings and streets, it turns out, are more fragile than the memories that inhabit them.

The civil war was triggered in 1975 by disagreements between Lebanon's Christians and Muslims over the presence and power of the Palestinian militias in Lebanon. The war would briefly stop in 1977 with the intervention of Arab forces led by Syria, only to resume again, this time with the participation of the Syrians on the side of the Palestinians and Muslims. After the Israelis invaded Lebanon in 1982 to support the Christians and expel the Palestinians, the war took on an international scope with a failed American and European military intervention. The period between 1983 and 1990 witnessed a rapid deterioration of the Lebanese economy and a series of wars between and among Christian and Muslim militias. It was not until a Saudi-brokered constitutional amendment evened out the distribution of power between Christians and Muslims—and until Desert Storm, when the United States reluctantly accepted Syrian hegemony over Lebanon—that the civil war officially came to an end in 1990.

The war displaced more than half of Lebanon's 3 million population and killed about 150,000. It also inflicted damage throughout the country and particularly in downtown Beirut, which stood as an evacuated demarcation area within the divided city throughout both the intensely violent and relatively quiet chapters of the war.

More than a decade after the war, the city center that had been largely razed for new development is slowly being filled up. The restoration work and new road networks have been completed. Judging by the crowds that swarm the restaurants and shops of the rebuilt quarters and by the high real estate prices, this revived district is a popular success. A residential neighborhood on the southeastern corner has also been restored, as have religious monuments. Based on the phasing of the master plan, the years between 2000 and 2008 were supposed to bring the most construction activity, exceeding 2 million square meters. Five years into this period, however, only a handful of new buildings have been added.

Significantly, Beirut is still looking for the shape of its old center and of the center's primary space, Martyrs Square. The proposed designs remain sketchy, and they vary from drawing to drawing in the technical plans and promotional brochures of Solidere, the private real estate holding company in charge of redevelopment. One drawing shows a broad perspective opening toward the sea to the north, highlighting this adjacency rather than activity in the Square. Another favors the smooth flow of traffic, transforming the Square into a boulevard. Yet another exaggerates the vegetation in the middle, turning it into a public garden. Based on the current or proposed uses, it is difficult to imagine a public space that could unify a mosque to its south, a Virgin megastore in its middle, and an archeological glacis on the north. Collective space seems no longer possible.

In the ten years since the launch of the plan to rebuild the city center, countless articles, books, and reports have been written opposing the clearing of downtown Beirut .[1] Many critics argue that razing about 85 percent of the buildings in the old center was unnecessary, especially as not all were damaged beyond repair. Critics also contend that handing over development to a private real estate company prevented average landowners and tenant citizens from participating in rebuilding. The massive clearing has been criticized for being economically grandiose and unrealistic, incommensurate with the city's capacities to actually develop the area. As in Hoda Barakat's novel, the clearing has been associated with the political and psychological amnesia that followed the war. Instead of reconciling their differences, the fighting factions and religious sects chose not to come to terms with their belligerent past but simply to switch from overt military to tacit confrontation.

01 Martyrs Square in its 1960s heyday. (Source: Aga Khan Trust for Culture. Michel Ecochard Archive)

The physical clearing bore out some of the fears of the early critics. The reconstruction has been expensive and has resulted in a dramatic drop in the value of Solidere's stock. It excluded average citizens and favored a more affluent clientele. The cleared area was simply too extensive to be filled up by an economy drained by international debt and exhausted by regional conflicts. Yet significant side effects resulting from this strategy of rebuilding are worth examining. Based on a study of the past ten years of reconstruction, I would argue that the process of refilling the physical void of downtown Beirut has itself generated unexpected patterns of development that may be as important in the shaping of the postwar city as the reconstruction plans. These patterns are similar to those that have guided much of the construction in the rest of Beirut, both after the war and throughout its modern history. Equally unexpected has been the way the reconstruction of downtown provides a platform on which contending claims over urban life are played out—even if the process of reconstruction has eliminated many of the old players. In the absence of an open political arena, the competing claims serve to revive political discourse, even if they are made on the grounds of aesthetics or urban development rather than sectarian dogma.

Once the downtown was cleared for redevelopment, the debate moved to determining the degree of restoration of the center. The plans prepared by Dar al-Handasah, a large corporate design firm, and ratified by the Lebanese parliament for implementation by Solidere, were supposed to be final, but they tended to emphasize regulation over form. They also deferred many key decisions to individual developers and left it up to them to negotiate their way with Solidere, the supervisor of the plan's execution. Even matters of historic preservation, which appeared at first to be clear and straightforward, were open for such negotiations.

02 The plan of Delahalle for Martyrs Square. (Source: Image courtesy of May Davie)

According to the plan, building essential infrastructure and restoring the salvaged buildings was to precede any new construction. As planning and legislation for reconstruction and transfer of property and development rights progressed in the early 1990s, numerous citizen groups were formed in response to the broad scope of change proposed by the plan. Many of these groups called for the restoration of the city as it was before the war. Amsterdam and Antwerp were evoked as models when the feasibility of such an undertaking was questioned. Such total restoration of the pre-trauma city met considerable opposition from the plan's supporters, who argued that Beirut—now a fragmented and overextended metropolis—needed a larger center and that the congestion and traffic problems had to be solved.

When the traffic engineers announced plans for wider roads, developers for larger parcels, and archeologists for deeper pits, it became evident that a total restoration of the center was going to be impossible. Even the number of structures to be restored dropped to fewer than 15 percent of the historic building stock. Parameters for preservation were set based on photographic and other forms of available documentation, but it soon became clear that Beirut had multiple and competing pasts. To which of these would the restoration efforts be anchored? Many downtown buildings changed over time, and many of those chosen for preservation—generally located in two districts dating back to the French mandate (1918–43)—were not as architecturally interesting as the preservationists claimed. As a result, the restored buildings and streets were overdecorated with references to a variety of pasts—sometimes to pasts they never actually had. Interestingly, the few new buildings constructed during this first phase also bore the impact of this historicism and were forced to mimic the preserved buildings, however false.

Recollection of the war itself—the painful but necessary process of social healing—is what the urban planners and architects neglected to respond to, according to many critics and citizen groups. A small park, known as the Garden of Forgiveness, was forced to absorb all the pressure of remembering the war in the downtown.

The rest of the district lacks any such references. On the other hand, it is difficult to imagine how such a longing for remembrance might be translated into built form without turning macabre or reducing architecture to sentimental scenography. The task is made even more difficult given the implicit political moratorium against a historical assessment of the war. Among the arts, the novel, and occasionally cinema and video art, have tackled the emotional and psychological remnants of war much more effectively than have architecture and urban design. In confronting these ghosts, many novels have taken either epic or documentary form.

Paradoxically, the amnesia of Beirut's postwar physical reconstruction has helped provide historical continuity between the city's defining myths: the myth of self-consumption and the myth of self-renewal. Since the formation of the nation of Lebanon in 1920, after the Versailles Treaty attached the Mount Lebanon region to the coastline on the west and the Bekaa Valley on the east, Beirut has seduced mountain peoples with its cosmopolitanism and permissive, liberal culture. The French mandate rulers envisioned Beirut as the main port of the country, but not as its capital. It was as if they feared the eventual consumption of the mountain by the city.

Despite its religious, sectarian, and regional overtones, the civil war has been interpreted by several revisionist historians as a struggle between Beirut and the countryside, the urban and the rural, or the cosmopolitan and the national. Before the war, nobody came from Beirut, but everybody yearned to go there. Like New York, Beirut refers only to itself. But such self-indulgence is ultimately punished. According to this common moralistic view, the war was a punishment for the excesses of self-consumption that endowed Beirut with seductive appeal and notoriety. Beirut's self-consumption, the foundational problem of Lebanon, presents a necessary condition for the cyclical myth to be realized.

The second defining myth asserts that Beirut will rise from the ashes. Popular songs and poetry reassured citizens in their makeshift shelters that the city would be rebuilt. Even the warlords who were serving the myth of self-consumption always insisted that the phoenix would eventually rise.

The myth of self-destruction feeds the myth of resilience. Yet a historical survey of this cycle quickly reveals that most of the calamities in the history of Beirut were natural, not man-made. Equally important, the transition from destruction to construction has rarely been the responsibility of the same generation. Sudden turning points that appear in the historical narratives of other cities confirm that a radical, if momentary, clearing of the air is necessary for the same generation to make its way from mortar guns to mortarboards. War criminals were exonerated by a general amnesty in 1991, which by absolving everybody enabled the country to move on. It is not surprising that it is mostly young video artists and novelists and returning expatriates who are taking on the responsibility of recollection, not those who were active during the war years. Amnesty and amnesia share more than an etymological root.

Over the past ten years of reconstruction, amnesia played another historical role, again manifesting itself urbanistically. The clearing of downtown created a collective homesickness for Beirutis, even those who still resided in Beirut. All manner of sentimentalized recollection was unleashed. Numerous coffeetable books were published, covering the different periods of the city's history.[2] Memoirs of the "good old days" appeared, along with fictional accounts of life in the city center. Relics salvaged from the clearing—old doors, decorative railings, column capitals—found new life as part of the decor of homes and restaurants.

Literary critic Svetlana Boym distinguishes between two kinds of nostalgia, *restorative* and *reflective*. The restorative form seeks the truth in recovering what has been lost. Boym describes this as an undertaking that tends to be associated with the rise of nationalist, often oppressive, regimes. The moratorium on history may have spared Beirut this form of nostalgia, allowing the reflective form to prevail. Reflective nostalgia favors fragmentary, selective, and highly personal attributes in the recovery of lost places. Here, individual architects selectively express personal accounts of the past—a past, Boym argues, that is devoid of politics. Whereas restorative nostalgia fetishizes the past, the reflective form makes possible a grassroots, collective process of recovery. In Beirut, individual developers and religious groups that reclaimed and restored their buildings operated largely in this manner. All parties have managed to evade the overbearing and ultimately untenable responsibility of "truthful" recovery. Instead, alternative histories were created through highly individuated, freely applied motifs: a hyper-Moorish style verging on Indian; an arabesque baroque; a Mamluk vernacular; and other novel fusions. Amnesia, it turns out, allowed a playful mingling of multiple, competing histories. It also passed along the responsibility of recovery from a central authority to a diverse array of architects, decorators, and artisans.

03 The new commercial center proposed by Michel Ecochard in 1964. (Source: Aga Khan Trust for Culture. Michel Ecochard Archive)

These side effects of nostalgia would seem peculiar to postwar reconstruction, but a survey of the history of the city's center reveals that these patters were evident in the past, in a series of contests between groups over the center and the major urban spaces associated with it.

Martyrs Square makes its historical appearance in late seventeenth- century drawings and literature as a clearing outside the walls of the city to the east, a caravan-staging place. This kind of loosely defined open space, known in Arabic as a *maidan,* also provided a visual clearing that aided defense of the city from invaders. As the city grew beyond its walls in the nineteenth century, the *maidan* slowly transformed into a large urban square. Given the density of the inner city and the rapid pace of development to its east and south, the Square soon emerged as the center of business and transportation activity. A road linking the city to Damascus was later constructed connecting the southern tip of the Square to the countryside.

In the late nineteenth century, Ottoman modernization initiatives accelerated Beirut's rise, enabling the city to become the main port on the eastern Mediterranean. These initiatives included introducing electricity and water networks as well as building wider roads in the old city. With the help of local donations, the Ottoman ruler of Beirut also transformed the Square into a major public garden. Its primacy in the city was formalized by the building of the Petit Serail—the new government quarters—on its northern side. The tramway lines introduced at the beginning of the twentieth century intersected in the Square and further altered the space.

The name of the Square changed often during this period, but the assassination of Arab nationalists there by the Ottoman military during World War I gave it its current name. Significantly, some of the old names, mostly the *Bourj* or *Balad,* are still used for the same square. The armistice brought the four- hundred-year Ottoman rule to an end and yielded a new nation-state called Greater Lebanon under the supervision of the French. An international trade fair at the beginning of the mandate was held in the Square as well as in an area just west of it, where the Ottomans had cleared part of the medieval fabric for an avenue they never built. The French eventually shaped this area into a small plaza with radiating streets and baptized it Place de l'Etoile.

But even after l'Etoile and the abutting parliament were built, Martyrs Square continued to function as a multiplicity of urban spaces. It provided the formal grounds in front of the government headquarters as well as the public

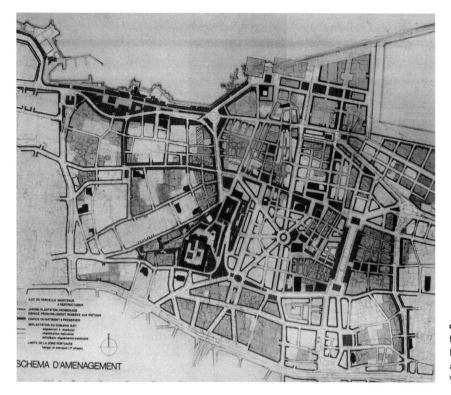

SCHEMA D'AMENAGEMENT

04 The APUR plan of 1977, the first "return" to the centrality of Martyrs Square. (Source: APUR and the Ministry of Public Works, Lebanon)

garden; it served as a transportation hub for Beirut's citizens; it provided accommodations for visitors and cafes for politicians and intellectuals. The Square also created a convenient buffer between the city's red-light district on one side and its major religious buildings on the other. But this eclectic collage of functions ultimately spawned competing claims over the city center and the Square; in the process, the different functions of the space were gradually eliminated while its symbolic role increased.

The French mandate did not propose major changes to the form of the city center until 1932, when the combined effects of a modern new port in Haifa and the Great Depression threatened Beirut's economy. The Brothers Danger, a French planning group, were asked to put together a master plan for the city that would support economic recovery based on trade and the seaport. Danger proposed the creation of different urban centers for the extramural neighborhoods of the city and a ring road to connect these centers to each other and to Martyrs Square. A further articulation of the plan of the square prepared by French architect Delahalle removed the Ottoman Serail, opened its northern face to the sea, and cascaded the square toward the port, the source of economic vitality. Delahalle also proposed Phoenician facades for the buildings abutting the Square. References to the Phoenicians abound in this period, as the nascent nation searched for ways to ground and justify itself historically. Much of the new architecture of the period would also replace the Levantine motifs with Moorish and Egyptian ones and would attempt to reclaim a national—as opposed to a regional—architecture. Although neither Danger's plans nor Delahalle's designs would be implemented, the connection to the sea remained a goal for many subsequent plans.

A study prepared in 1942 by French planner Michel Ecochard shifted from shaping spaces to laying out networks. In his correspondence with the French authorities during World War II, Ecochard emphasized the need to create an open network of circulation between the city's main port and airport, bypassing the city center and its main square, to facilitate quick mobilization of troops in the event of an Axis invasion. Ecochard's plan remained mostly at the level of road networks, but his side projects included a literal bypass in the form of a multilevel road to the north of the Square. With this bypass, Martyrs Square lost its transportation function. As in the Danger plan, the Square also lost its administrative role, this time to a new government complex to be located between the Place de l'Etoile and Serail Hill to the west.

Ecochard's plan inspired some of new roads built in the 1950s, in the process planting the seeds of urban decentralization. A more explicit attempt to move the administration out of the center (and out of the city) came from a report by the Greek planner Constantinos Doxiadis in 1959. Doxiadis proposed creating a new administrative center for Beirut outside the city's municipal boundaries, where the road to Damascus intersected with the peripheral road. Rather than revise the layout of the old center, the government of the time opted for the creation of an altogether new administrative capital away from the city and closer to the country. This move followed a short but serious civil war in 1958 that brought about numerous confrontations between the state and the opposition in the city center. In the end only the presidential palace moved out of the city, but the resultant vacancy would often be taken for a vacuum to be filled by competing powers.

In 1963, Ecochard was brought back to Lebanon to propose a master plan for the metropolitan district of Beirut. This time he envisioned a new modern city south of Beirut that would release pressure from the traditional old city. He also proposed the creation of a new business center south of Martyrs Square that would draw business out of the center and place it between the old and new city. Whereas the plan for a new city would eventually be abandoned, the drive for decentralization gained momentum in subsequent years and culminated in the emergence of a new business center in the Hamra area near the American University of Beirut.

In parallel, an infatuation with the possibility of reclaiming Martyrs Square preoccupied Beirutis. With the removal of the Serail, the Square acquired a much larger statue commemorating the martyrs. A constant reworking of the landscape in the Square and of the layout of bus and taxi stops attests to the increasing presence of the Square in the popular imagination, even if its urban functions were reduced. In the later 1960s and early 1970s the Square became the location of many increasingly violent student and labor demonstrations. Grassroots movements and political parties were filling the power vacuum created by the weak state.

A radical inversion of this decentralization tendency took place after the 1975–77 war episode. During a brief lull in fighting in 1977, a plan was proposed calling for reconstruction of the city center. Authored by the French planning agency APUR and strongly preservationist in tone, this scheme concentrated on highlighting and manicuring the city's open spaces. Interestingly, the plan called for Martyrs Square (which reacquired its role as *maidan*, a clearing between East and West Beirut, during the war) to be furnished with trees and wide sidewalks, as if offering the citizens a space in which their differences could be peacefully played out.

The war resumed soon afterward, but the downtown—particularly Martyrs Square—continued to play an important role in maintaining the image of the city as a coherent entity. Despite its division into two parts (and its subsequent splintering into even smaller ones), the center became like the Forbidden City in Beijing, holding the city together symbolically by the power of its ubiquitous image and its inaccessibility.

The end of the war in 1990 and the Dar al-Handasah/Solidere plan brought the city back to its center. Governmental institutions rushed back; so did the religious groups. Businesses, particularly larger ones, are slowly returning to the center, and glittery restaurants and shops are crowding the streets and sidewalks. But the role of the center in relation to the rest of the city—especially at the levels of business, transportation, and public life—remains unclear. This lack of clarity is most glaring in Martyrs Square. Against the backdrop of the restored neighborhood, this clearing now serves as spillover parking, exhibition or concert space, or a site for unsophisticated art installations. It seems to have returned to its previous role as a vital void, as a *maidan,* outside the downtown. Absorbing speculation about urban development, while resisting being taken over by any one idea, has been one of the most vital, albeit unrecognized, functions of this public space.

A major dynamic in urban development in Lebanon is based on the fact that the value of land is often much higher than the value of the buildings that sit on it. While building location and size do figure prominently in the evaluation of property, the historical value of the building does not contribute greatly to the overall assessment of the property. Given a very weak mortgage market, real estate in Lebanon is not linked to the fluctuations in interest rates. Moreover, property taxes are low. Investment and speculation in real estate can continue even if the demand is not high, because real estate still provides the most secure sector for investment. It was therefore not surprising when planners proposed 4.7 million square meters of built up area in downtown Beirut, including 2 million square meters to house 40,000 inhabitants.

With a building code that keeps getting revised to increase land exploitation, especially in the business districts, it is difficult to see how the urban fabric can hold steady against this kind of change. Buildings dating back to the early 1950s and 1960s are routinely torn down and replaced by parking lots, as owners play a waiting game with prospective developers. These clearings serve as development indices, particularly in neighborhoods like Ras Beirut and Ashrafieh, where competing claims and scenarios for development help increase the value of the vacated property as well as the properties around it.

Another example of erratic development in the downtown area is the reconstruction of the old souks. Most downtown development is supposed to be handled by private developers who purchase land from Solidere and build it up according to Solidere's plan. However, Solidere has reserved for itself the right to build on about 25 percent of the land, including key sites that would serve as seed projects to encourage development around them. One of these key sites was the souks project—the reconstruction of the city's old bazaar, located just south of the historic harbor. Given unanticipated political changes and financial difficulties, the project was halted for four years, during which most of the sites around it continued to be purchased and built on by private developers—despite economic stagnation and the absence of a pilot project. Although anticipation of the revitalized souks has not triggered as much

05 Dar al-Handasah 1996 Master Plan for Beirut Central District. (Source: Solidere)

development as their realization would have, speculative development has clearly overwhelmed rational planning and may require changes in the land uses of the new bazaar. The clearing around Martyrs Square may be interpreted as a larger version of this pattern in Beirut's development culture, particularly in the way it affords extraordinary view corridors.

These patterns of development are not unique to the postwar period, nor are they unique to downtown Beirut. However, given the limited political platform in Beirut after the war, and the highly charged location of the downtown in the country's geopolitics, they prove that urban life can overcome exclusionary practices. Today, the main political questions are being asked through means other than religious sectarianism or party politics. When interrogated carefully, the city's built environment, architectural heritage, and public space, expose a highly political content that can still be debated and challenged.

The political theorists Ernesto Laclau and Chantal Mouffe have argued that the dynamics of democratic politics stem from the fact that the central position of power remains open for contest. The center is constantly cleared and kept at an equal distance from everybody's reach in order for democracy to maintain the potential for constant debate and change. The physical voids produced by the speculative development culture in Beirut may not fully correspond to this operative void in democratic politics; furthermore, urban spaces cannot be totally fluid if they are to maintain their public role. However, the constant redefinition of Martyrs Square over its recent history asserts that Beirut's development culture and its political life intersect at many unexpected points. Much of the Square's resilience and vitality can be explained by its constant change rather than through an examination of its salient features. In opposition to plans for Martyrs Square that limit its role by fixing its shape and function, architects and urban designers today are challenged to imagine ways in which the vitality of constant change might be enhanced and reified by design. In this, perhaps, lies the key to the continued resilience of downtown Beirut.

Notes
This essay is reprinted with permission from *The Resilient City: How Modern Cities Recover from Disaster*, edited by Lawrence J. Vale and Thomas J. Campanella (New York and Oxford: Oxford University Press, 2004).
1. See, for example, Nabil Beyhum, *Reconstruire Beyrouth, Les Paris sur le Possible* (Lyon: Maison de l'Orient, Etudes sur le Monde Arab, no. 5, 1991); Peter G. Rowe and Hashim Sarkis, eds., *Projecting Beirut: Episodes in the Construction and Reconstruction of a Modern City* (Munich: Prestel, 1998); and Samir Khalaf, *Beirut Reclaimed* (Beirut: Dar An-Nahar, 1993).
2. See, for example, Fouad Debbas, *Beirut, Our Memory* (Beirut: Naufal Group, 1986); Ghassan Tueni and Fares Sassine, eds., *El Bourj: Place de la Liberte et Porte du Levant* (Beirut: Dar An-Nahar, 2000); and Fares Sassine and Nawaf Salam, eds., *Liban, Le Siecle en Image* (Beirut: Dar An-Nahar, 2000).

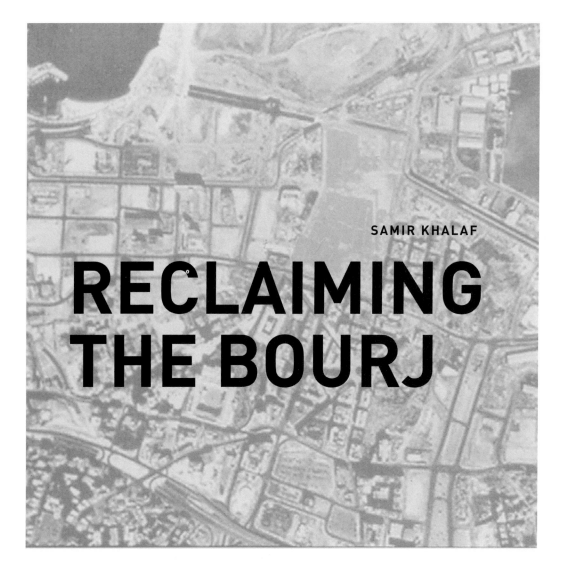

SAMIR KHALAF

RECLAIMING
THE BOURJ

Archeological findings repeatedly show that Beirut's central square has served as a home for humans almost since their appearance on earth. Indeed, some of the stone implements found on the site may be traced to the Lower Paleolithic period, 2 or 3 million years ago. Yet despite its impressive history, the Square's emergence as a cosmopolitan urban center is of relatively recent vintage. In fact, the most definitive signs of urbanization—rural influx and the overflow of the population beyond its medieval walls—did not appear in substantial form until the 1860s. Of course there were earlier signs of rural exodus. Dislocation in native crafts, a decline in silk production, and a shift in the pattern of trade, particularly during the Egyptian occupation (1831–41), had prompted population movement toward coastal towns. These and even earlier movements, however, were limited in scale. For example, when Volney visited Beirut in 1773, he described it as a small town with not more than 6,000 people. There was not any perceptible increase in the population during the next six decades; by 1830, the population was still in the neighborhood of 8,000.

The decade of Egyptian presence, with its concomitant commercialization and opening up of Mount Lebanon to western incursions, added only another 2,000 to Beirut's population. This relatively slow rate of increase (about 500 people annually) was maintained during the 1840s and 1850s. In short, it was not until the outbreak of civil disturbances in the late 1850s and early 1860s that the impact of a massive shift in population began to be felt. Beirut's population leaped from 22,000 in 1857 to 70,000 in 1863. In the short span of August–September 1860, local Anglo-Saxon missionaries gave aid to more than 20,000 refugees in Beirut (Jessup 1910: 251).

All descriptions of Beirut prior to the 1860s attest to the fact that it was no more than a small fortified medieval town with seven main gates, surrounded by gardens. The city was built around its historic port, with defenses on the landward side and two towers at the entrance of the port. As in most European towns before industrialization, people in Beirut lived, worked, and carried on nearly all their daily routines within the same urban quarter. Ethnic and religious affiliations created relatively homogeneous and compact residential neighborhoods. Gross density was high—around 300 people per hectare—giving the town an overwhelming impression of congestion. The French poet Lamartine, who visited Beirut in 1832, observed that the roofs of some houses served as terraces of others. Except for souks, khans, baths, places of worship, and other public buildings that dominated the town, the prevailing house types were flat-roofed farmhouses and the traditional two- or three-storied, red-tiled villas with elaborate facades and decorative railed stairways and balconies. Sandstone blocks, quarried in the area, were the predominant construction material. Lush subtropical vegetation graced the well-tended gardens of houses and lined winding alleyways.

The alleys were soon converted to paved streets. Construction leaped beyond the medieval walls of the city to absorb the persistent inflow of rural migrants. The construction of the wharf in Beirut's port in 1860 to accommodate increasing maritime traffic, like other infrastructure developments and public amenities developed throughout the second half of the nineteenth century (e.g., harbor facilities, Damascus railway, gas lights, potable water, electric tramways, telegraph and postal services, quarantine facilities, dispensaries and hospitals, along with schools, colleges, and printing houses) assisted naturally in the expansion and urbanization of Beirut. As a residence for consul-generals, headquarters for French, American, and British missions, and growing center of trade and services, the city gradually began to attract a cosmopolitan and heterogeneous population.

In Beirut's eventful past, much like its most recent history, three distinct but related elements stand out: First, the predisposition of the Bourj—as the center was known—to incorporate and reconcile pluralistic and multicultural features; second, the center's inventiveness in reconstituting and refashioning its collective identity and public image; and third, its role in hosting and disseminating popular culture, consumerism, mass entertainment and often, unsavory tourist attractions. I will elaborate on each to elucidate how they might inform plans for reconstituting the Bourj as the iconic image of Beirut's future. But first, it is instructive to provide a brief sketch of the city's checkered history with urban planning.

THE ENDEMIC FAILURE OF SUCCESSIVE URBAN PLANNING SCHEMES

The decades between the two world wars were dense with public and private construction. They were also marked by early efforts to introduce a modicum of urban planning and zoning. For example, in 1928 new property laws were enacted providing freedom in the use of private property; this was meant to annul the Ottoman edict that had restricted building on farmland. Two architectural icons graced the still

1841 The Square as maidan located outside the walls of the city. (All maps prepared by students in Square One studio)

tame city-space of Beirut. The Place de L'Etoile, the most visible instance of grandiose French urban planning, was superimposed over the destroyed area of the old city. The Parliament building was constructed on one of the Beaux-Arts grids that surrounded the Square. This was intended to serve as a symbolic national setting—the seat of government radiating its political primacy over the recently extended borders of Greater Lebanon (Gavin 1998: 218–219). The other two eastern wedges of the L'Etoile, intended as a star-shaped design in the original scheme, are obstructed by the presence of three prominent religious edifices: Greek Orthodox and Greek Catholic churches and the historic Nuriyyeh Shrine (see Davie 2003). The second architectural landmark was the Hotel St. George built by the Societe des Grands Hotels du Mandats. Antoine Thabet, a French-trained Lebanese architect, designed a modern, minimalist concrete structure that has served as a secular national emblem of the myth-shrouded cove on which it is gracefully perched. (Legend has it that this was where St. George slayed the dragon.) More tangibly, the St. George acted as the anchor for the hotel district that ultimately dominated the skyline of the city.

Early in the 1930s, French High Commissioner de Martel freed the Lebanese government of its burdensome debt and channeled the funds to public works projects instead, particularly port facilities, public buildings, and road networks. In 1932, the first master plan for Beirut, the work of the French urban consultant Danger, was not approved by the government. The plan had proposed major axes of circulation, building regulations, and land-use studies. It also recommended that neighboring suburbs and villages be incorporated in future planning schemes. Rather than implementing the plan, however, the government sought to legislate procedures for approving building permits and construction. Another French architect and urban designer, Delahalle, presented a flamboyant design for the reembellishment of downtown Beirut and the Bourj Square. The plan, perhaps inspired by Beirut's Phoenician site, proposed opening up the place des Canons to the harbor by devising a massive terraced space. Like its predecessor, the plan was never enacted.

During World War II, Beirut miraculously was spared what seemed at the time as likely destruction. As Germany

1876 The Square demarcated by the road to Damascus with the trace of the wall and the new neighborhoods east of Beirut.

invaded France, all mandated countries fell under the command of the Vichy government. Beirutis, fearing that the famine of World War I might be repeated, started fleeing to surrounding mountain towns and villages. The pleading of President Alfred Naccache to declare Beirut an open city was heeded by the Vichy troops in control of the city at the time.

Another master plan, this time by Michel Ecochard, a prominent French specialist on Middle Eastern urban planning, was introduced in 1944. Despite its shortcomings, the plan was the first attempt to incorporate the sprawling suburbs—from Nahr al-Mout in the North to Ouzai in the South—into the scheme. It also envisaged a second major axis within the city, running East-West perpendicular to the Damascus Road. It also provided the first comprehensive study of land-use and zoning, proposing to distinguish industrial and commercial outlets from residential zones (for further details, see Salam 1993).

The failure to implement Ecochard's proposals was compounded by the influx of the first wave of Palestinian refugees, who initially settled in Beirut's southern outskirts. Eventually they moved to refugee camps in Sabra, Shatila, and Burj al-Barajneh in the southern suburbs and in Qarantina and Tel al-Zaatar in the north and northeast. By 1975, the number of Palestinian refugees was estimated at 300,000. The Egli planning report of 1950, cognizant of demographic pressures and mounting urbanization, was the first plan to receive government approval. This was promptly followed by the Plan Directeur de Beyrouth (1951–54), which adopted most of the proposals of Ecochard and Egli (see Khalaf 1985).

The experience of Doxiadis Associates, a firm commissioned in May 1957 by the U.S. Operations Mission and the Government of Lebanon to prepare a long-term "Ekistics Program" for Lebanon, is instructive. This massive survey, unique in Lebanon's history, involved a comprehensive review (both visual and analytical) of the entire country. It employed novel quantitative and qualitative strategies to depict the spatial features of the built environment, its architectural character, housing types, public squares, souks—even profiles of the facial expressions of common people. The study relied on personal notes, ethnographic material, and tape-recorded impressions. Despite the formidable data amassed, however, the

1914 The Square with the new Ottoman municipal building, the new tram lines, and the public garden.

survey fell short of producing any rigorous designs or grounded projects, but the civil disturbances of 1958 might have been partly responsible. Altogether it remained schematic in its proposals and perspectives, though some of these were subsequently incorporated in the Ecochard plans of 1963. Despite its shortcomings, the survey can still be considered a valuable undertaking because it provided proof of the potential of planning to operate independently of political regimes. (For further substantiation, see Sarkis 1998 and 2004.)

Construction of the Camille Chamoun Cite Sportive to host the Mediterranean games (1956) and the completion of the new International Airport in Khaldeh both served to stretch the city limits further south, beyond the boundaries of municipal Beirut. All subsequent attempts, particularly the stern planning policies enforced against laissez-faire urbanism during President Chihab's tenure (1958–64), failed to curb the incessant inflow of rural migration.

In 1963, the General Directorate of Urban Planning and the Higher Council for Urban Planning (HCUP) were created to advise the president. The IRFED report, a comprehensive survey of the demographic, health, socioeconomic, educational, and cultural resources of the country, was published. Michel Ecochard served as consultant to the General Director of Urban Planning and played a part in producing the second master plan: Plan Directeur de Beyrouth et des Banlieues. The plan called for the creation of a new modern city contiguous to the congested old city. It also provided a new detailed building code for the city, suburbs, and country as a whole.

Lebanon, and Beirut in particular, was never short of blueprints; the devil was always in the details of implementation. Hence there has always been a wasteful discrepancy between audacious planning on one hand and executive ineffectiveness on the other. This tendency is particularly visible in the failure of repeated urban schemes to curb some of the unsettling consequences of rural exodus and the unplanned and uncontrolled growth of Beirut into a major city (Khalaf 1985).

The relentless inflow of displaced rural migrants into Beirut was compounded by two regional and global forces. First, the growth of agro-business brought about a significant

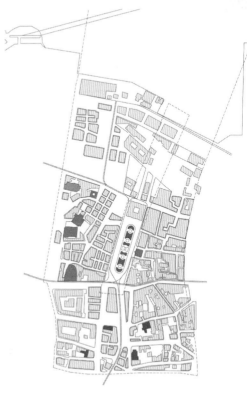

post-1921 The Square as part of the 1921 international fair grounds and the new Debbas Square to the south

decline in sharecropping, the traditional lifeline of Lebanese farming. Whereas small farmers and sharecroppers constituted about 25 percent of the active agricultural population in 1950, the proportion dropped sharply to not more than 5 percent in 1970. Displaced farmers were forced to either migrate or be reduced to the status of wage laborers. Both options were equally unappealing. Migrants became part of the pauperized "misery belt" of Beirut's suburbs. Those Lebanese compelled to become wage laborers had to suffer the indignities of competing with the cheap pool of itinerant labor made up mostly of Palestinian and Syrian refugees.

Second, the growing insecurity of border villages because of incessant Israeli incursions generated waves of outmigration. Results of the only national manpower survey (undertaken in 1970) revealed that nearly one-fifth of Lebanon's rural population during the 1960s had migrated to Beirut's suburban fringe. Exodus from the south was as high as one-third (see Nasr 1978: 9-10 for further details). Little wonder that by the early 1970s such displaced and disgruntled groups became a support base for political radicalization.

The population of metropolitan Beirut had reached 1 million by 1970—approximately 45 percent of the country's population concentrated in a surface area of barely 2 percent. The last attempt to right this imbalance before the outbreak of collective strife was in 1973. The *Livre Blanc* (White Book) proposed a new master plan that supported decentralization. By then, however, it was too late.

Several factors, embedded in Lebanon's sociopolitical culture, account for the repeated failure of urban planning schemes. First, the process of rational urban planning has always been undermined by the persistence of clientelistic politics and other forms of patronage. These allow strategically placed individuals to control the distribution of benefits by manipulating zoning laws and ordinances. Political connections enable speculation associated with anticipated planning or rezoning schemes, and even ordinary citizens can sometimes secure favored treatment or protection from the law. Second, the deep-seated weakness of state agencies and the consequent deficiency in civic-mindedness and public consciousness—all of which have direct implications for urban planning—are pronounced. The Lebanese state, compared to primary communal and other allegiances, has

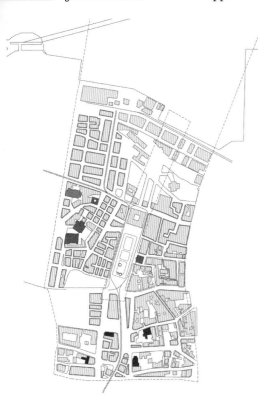

1933 The Square with a new garden in the middle

always been an enfeebled institution. Likewise, as a fragmented political culture, Lebanon has experienced a high incidence of civil unrest and social disorder. The rampant chaos and lawlessness generated by such protracted episodes renders law enforcement difficult. Furthermore, when normlessness becomes so widespread, offenses such as the confiscation of property and violation of construction and zoning ordinances become relatively minor transgressions (for further substantiation, see Khalaf 1985).

Finally, Lebanon's experience with urban planning reveals a poignant paradox—a dissonance between the rather orderly regulation of private space in homes, neighborhoods, and quarters and the almost total disregard for public space. These dissonant attitudes toward the private and public spheres are clearly both symptoms and sources of the deficiency in civic-mindedness that pervades society. They provide challenges that must be addressed in transforming the Bourj into a public sphere.

The story of Beirut's destruction, particularly the repeated devastation and looting of its center, is likewise riddled with anomalies. The fiercest battles, displaying the most barbarous cruelties, took place there, as if the historic hub of the old city were both the most coveted and most maligned space. The center had more than just logistical and economic values: to gain control of the center offered the opportunity to reclaim its contested identity and redefine its future.

Hence it was not coincidental that the early rounds of fighting in 1975–76 started for control of the city's center and then extended to the hotel districts and the southeastern suburbs. The creation of the infamous "Green Line" along the Damascus Road divided Beirut in two: the predominantly Muslim West Beirut and the predominantly Christian East Beirut. The social geography of the city evolved to form exclusive communities. In quick succession, all the Muslim enclaves in East Beirut (i.e. Qarantina, Nabaa, Tel al-Zaatar) were destroyed. In a parallel fashion, the Ouzai coastline on the southern suburbs and private beaches were all overtaken by squatters. Similar pressures encroached on areas such as Raouche and Hamra. One inevitable byproduct of the early round of fighting was decentralization. Secondary suburban districts and towns mushroomed

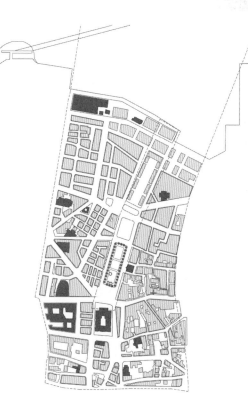

1935 The Delahalle plan showing terraces towards the sea.

on both sides of the divide: Jdeideh, Daoura, Zalka, Maamiltayn, and Junieh to the east; Lailaki, Hayy al-Silloum, and up to Saida to the south.

The brief and deceptive lull in the intensity of fighting in 1977 prompted the government to establish the Council for Development and Reconstruction (CDR) to plan and administer the reconstruction of the devastated central business district (CBD). A French consulting firm, L'Atelier Parisien d'Urbanism (APUR), was commissioned to produce the master plan for reconstruction. The conceptual framework of APUR's plan was informed by five compelling considerations: 1) to maintain, where possible, the original urban fabric as well as the preexisting tenure of property holding; 2) to encourage the legal owners and occupants of the CBD to return and reclaim their previous enterprises; 3) to facilitate the return of the CBD to its traditional role as a unifying and homogenizing setting for the country's multiconfessional composition; 4) to introduce the necessary infrastructural improvements to the CBD to expedite its rehabilitation; and 5), to revitalize badly damaged areas through the establishment of conventional real estate companies and the implementation of other strategies of postwar reconstruction (see Salam 1998: 129–130).

The reconstruction was barely under way when it had to be suspended because of renewed fighting. The CBD, along with certain quarters of Ashrafieh, were subjected to more destruction. With the Israeli invasion of 1982, the CBD was further damaged by heavy bombardment, along with the dense urban fabric between Martyrs Square and Souk Sursock.

Eager to launch the process of reconstruction, Oger Liban (a private Lebanese-Saudi company) ventured to take on the immense project of reconstructing the CBD. Oger commissioned Dar al-Handasah in 1983 to prepare a master plan for the project. The resumption of fighting, this time in the mountain regions, generated another influx of refugees into Beirut. The so-called Mountain War provoked a revolt against the government that led to further destruction in the southern suburbs and areas of Ras Beirut.

In 1986 yet another French "schema directeur" came into being. This time it was the joint product of CDR and the Higher Council of Urban Planning (HCUP) with APUR (the French agency) acting as principal consultant. The study proposed the first master plan for the entire metropolitan district of Beirut, with four satellite commercial centers in Dora, Hazmieh,

Lailaki, and Khaldeh.

During the de facto division of the country into a two-state system (1988–90), the dislocation between various regions and sectors became sharper. Anarchy grew as infighting among Christian militias developed into turf wars. Much of the satellite suburbs of Jdeideh, Dora, Hadath, and Hazmieh were destroyed.

The collapse of the two-state interlude ushered in the first concerted efforts of postwar reconstruction. The head of Oger Liban in Beirut was appointed director of the CBD. By 1991 a new master plan for the CBD, designed by Henri Edde of Dar al-Handasah, came into being. A decree law was legislated for the creation of a private real estate holding company (Solidere) to administer the reconstruction of the CBD.

No sooner than Solidere was created, however, than it was met with public outcry. Voices of dissent, particularly against some of the financial, economic, and legal implications of the privatization of reconstruction, became louder (see Salam 1998: 131–133). Public dissatisfaction extended to government departments entrusted to implement the plans, particularly those of HCUP and CBD. Within this contested setting, Bechtel Corporation was commissioned to produce a strategy for reconstruction with the collaboration of Dar al-Handasah. The plan relocated activities within the center to provide Beirut with a corporate, international image. Given the disruptive potential of displaced refugees, a new ministry for refugees was established to expedite the return of the displaced to their communities.

Nineteen ninety-two was an important year in Beirut's postwar history, marked by two contrasting but related circumstances. First, it saw the ominous influx of unanchored masses into the city center and adjoining quarters. Second, it heralded the poignant process of destroying the already savaged and neglected buildings and cityscape. The urban design project for the city center, the work of Dar al-Handasah, was approved with some modification by the Lebanese Parliament. UNESCO was granted the privilege of excavating and documenting the archeological heritage during the reconstruction period.

The dramatic launching of the process of rebuilding the cen-

1941 The 1941 Michel Ecochard proposal showing traffic bypass to the north of the square.

ter by bulldozing the relics of its historic core did not quell the heated public debate over the city's collective memory and its envisioned future image. Partisans on all sides had ample opportunity to air their views.

THE BOURJ AS AN OPEN AND HOMOGENIZING PLACE

The Bourj—more than its adjoining quarters and eventual outlying suburban districts—has always served as a vibrant and cosmopolitan melting pot of diverse groups and sociocultural transformations. While other neighborhoods and districts of the expanding city attracted distinct sectarian, ethnic, class, and ideological groups—and eventually evolved into segregated urban enclosures—the Bourj always managed to remain a fairly open and homogenizing space.

This receptivity to foreign cultures, competing educational missions, European trade, and an incessant inflow of goods, itinerant groups, and borrowed ideologies accounts for both its resonant pluralism and assimilating character. These two forces, pluralism and tolerance, became the defining elements of Beirut's center. This climate was evident during the first half of the nineteenth century. Partly because of the center's compact size and predominantly commercial character, the intermingling and collaboration between the various communities was both inevitable and vital for their survival. Typical of a so-called merchant republic, traders and entrepreneurs of various communities were partners in private business ventures who assisted each other in times of financial need. They perceived themselves as members of an urban merchant elite, resisting the hostile elements that threatened their common economic interests.

In the old souks and bazaars flanking the Bourj, artisans and traders worked side by side. Spatial segregation and the location of shops was determined by occupation, not religion. Much like the spatial layout of residential quarters elsewhere in the burgeoning city beyond the Bourj, the bazaars and retail outlets were strikingly uniform in their architectural features. On the whole, social interaction was characterized by goodwill, tolerance, and personal ties. Such cooperation was not confined to domestic and commercial relations; it spilled over into other spheres of public life. Christians and

1958 The Square showing the removal of the Petit Serail.

Muslims met at official functions and served on the same committees, courts, and tribunals. For example, during the period of national struggle against Ottoman repression and centralization of the Young Turks at the turn of the century (1880–1908), Christians and Muslims transcended their communal differences and participated collectively in underground political movements and secret societies.

Likewise, during the struggle for independence and subsequent mass demonstrations in support of labor unions, women's suffrage, Palestinian mobilization, and the rights of other dispossessed groups, the Bourj always served as rallying ground for neglected and marginalized segments of society. Student demonstrations, often with heightened confrontational strategies, reserved their most virulent expressions for the Bourj.

In the mandate era, the resort to such public spheres became more pronounced. Elizabeth Thompson (2000) identifies two structural forces underlying this change. First, the public sector underwent massive expansion with the growth of transport and communication services, schooling and health care, new entertainment venues such as cinemas and parks, and newspapers and magazines. Second, the public sphere was steadfastly emerging as a primary political arena, particularly in the 1930s when the Parliament was shut down by the French for half a decade. Mass demonstrations, market closures, even street battles became the modus operandi of the nascent postcolonial political culture. Urban notables mobilized their client groups in protest. Dissenting movements took the streets to voice their concerns. Turf battles with the French forces for control of urban space and the virtual public space (freedom of speech and media) became frequent.

Largely because of the Petit Serail (built in 1883), which served first as headquarters for the Ottoman postal service and later (1926–50) became the official "palace" for Lebanese presidents, the Bourj became the ultimate destination for all public demonstrations. Protests were legion in the 1940s, particularly demonstrations against poor living standards and in support of public sector workers seeking better pay.

One unusual feature of the Bourj accounts for the role it played as meeting place for various groups. At a time when telephone and other forms of mediated communication were nonexistent, the mushrooming hotels, pensions, locandas, and residences were used as transit stops and meeting grounds. A nascent hotel industry, as early as the 1830s, had already developed

Coffee shop near Martyrs Square at the turn of the century. (Source: Fouad Debbas Collection)

to accommodate the growing stream of foreign travelers. Travelers to the interior always sought to stop in Beirut en route. Travel accounts are lavish in their praise of the elegance of the hotels visitors encountered. Some of the graceful hotels, especially the locandas and casinos built and managed first by Greeks, Maltese, Italians, and then native Lebanese, came into being during the second half of the nineteenth century.

In the late 1920s, the number of hotels nearly doubled and continued to increase into the 1930s. The number of restaurants and bars also increased considerably during the same period (Thompson 2000: 179). Villagers frequenting the city had their own chains of residences and pensions; some of these premises became associated with particular villages. To groups awaiting ocean liners for their departure from Lebanon, these hotels became settings charged with drama.

Not only hotels but bus and car terminals, transport agencies, and coffeehouses served as meeting points. It was common for Beirut residents to deliver and receive their mail, messages, and parcels through such venues. To villagers seeking jobs, contacts, and other city amenities, these places became surrogate homes and offices.

1975 The Square as it existed before the 1975 Civil War.

This is the interlude in Beirut's urban history when displaced groups—largely because of the quickening pace of urbanization—felt the need to reconnect by seeking refuge in urban spaces amenable for such informal contacts. For example, at a time when clubs, galleries, auditoriums, and other formal public venues were still rare, coffeehouses, restaurants, and bars became lively domains for intellectuals, artists, poets, journalists, and politicians. As early as the 1930s, such places acquired notoriety as meeting spots for particular groups.

Even when public institutions such as the Lebanese Academy of Arts (ALBA), The Lebanese Cenacle, or Dar al-Fan established or relocated their premises during the 1940s, these alternative meting places did not lessen the popularity of the traditional venues. This coexistence of traditional outlets and more specialized, commercial, and corporate-like organizations continued throughout the post-independence period and beyond. Indeed, the accommodation of such "third spaces" was a distinctive attribute of the Bourj. The growth of secular associations throughout the 1960s and until the outbreak of hostilities in the mid-1970s did not displace the conventional shopkeepers, artisans, and neighborhood stores; they merely enriched the diversity of outlets. Hence seemingly disparate groups felt equally at home: the villager and regular neighborhood customer who sought familiarity and personal contacts, and the tourist in search of novelty and adventure.

REINVENTING IDENTITY AND PUBLIC IMAGE

Consistent with its evolving national character, the center has had several names, reflecting contested identities. The first urban form the Bourj assumed was *al maidan*, which prefigured its role as a common ground (public sphere) for unanchored social groups. It came to be identified with images of plains, meadows, grounds, or fields. In the term's original Persian context, it was primarily associated with pilgrims, traders, militias. As it found expression in other settings such as Cairo, Bombay, Ahmedabad, and Calcutta, the word embraced other elements and uses. Throughout, however, the idea of *maidan* emerged as a result of human intervention directed toward keeping land free and indeterminate, and hence negotiable. It should not therefore be confused with enclosed courtyards or cultivated parks, yet nor is it a desolate wilderness. Rather, as Mathur (1999) suggested, it is somewhere in between. It is in fact close to what Ivan Illich calls "commons":

> that part of the environment that lay beyond a person's own threshold and outside his own possession, but to which, however, that person had a recognized claim of usage—not to produce commodities but to provide for the subsistence of kin. Neither wilderness nor home is commons, but that part of the environment for which customary law exacts specific forms of community respect. (Illich 1982: 18)

A striking feature of the *maidan* that is of particular relevance to the Bourj's emergence and metamorphosis is its predisposition to embrace a diversity of cultures while containing measures of neutrality and anonymity. As Mathur puts it:

> In cities of increasingly circumscribed social, racial, or economic enclaves, the *maidan* has come to both symbolize and provide neutral

territory, a ground where people can gather on a common plane. It is a place that offers freedom without obligation. This ability to accommodate a diverse range of social and political structures makes the *maidan* an extremely significant space in the city. It is a place where people can touch the spirit of commonness. (Mathur 1999: 215)

Given the scarcity and inevitable competition for the use of precious urban space, a reappropriation of a *maidan* in its original concept or form is unlikely in central Beirut. Its underlying spirit and sentiment, however, are still realizeable. Indeed, because of the disappearance of many historical *maidans*, efforts are being made today to appropriate landscapes that lend themselves to both settled and transient elements. Hence open spaces made available for urban redevelopment provide rare and challenging opportunities for urban designers. Open spaces can offer the chance to reclaim a measure of freedom and spontaneity within the enclosure of the city. Adjoining areas radiating from Beirut's center are increasingly commodified, deliberately monitored, and exploited in ways bound to discourage spontaneous appropriation or unplanned development. Within such seemingly impervious constraints, urbanists and landscape architects are seeking to promote indeterminacy and open-mindedness.

The *maidan's* lifespan was short. No sooner had itinerant groups started settling within and adjoining the remains of the fortified medieval embankments than the Bourj became *Sahat al-Sour*. In 1773 the imperial Russian fleet installed artillery on its elevated fortifications—hence the appellation *Place de Canons*. By 1860, it was the imperial canons of the French fleet that reinforced that label. Prior to that and for a brief interlude (after 1850) when Beirut's center was largely desolate except for the few bedouins from the interior who occupied one of its remaining fortified towers, it bore the designation *Sahat Bourj el Kachef*.

By 1863, the Beirut-Damascus Road was completed, strengthening the link with Damascus and the territory beyond Mount Lebanon and the coast. The centrality of the Bourj was further reinforced. A tolled caravan route extended from Bourj Square in a valley between the Ashrafieh area and the Western regions of Moussaytbeh and Mazraa. Under Dawud Pasha (1861–68), the streets of Beirut were widened and paved to accommodate carriages of the French Damascus Road Company.

During the Mutesarrifate, the Municipal Council of Beirut launched a series of magisterial projects. Unlike in other Ottoman provinces, private initiative and foreign capital contributed heavily to changing the urban landscape, particularly in the wake of the economic boom during the last decade or so of the nineteenth century. Initiated at that time, this form of private intervention in the regulation of public space became a recurrent feature. For example, as early as 1879, when Fakhry Bek launched his landscaping project of the public garden in the Bourj, about thirty families contributed to the effort.

This *Muntazah*, as it was initially labeled, became the edifying centerpiece of the Bourj. Perhaps because of its novelty and the patrons it drew from a cross- section of society, the Bourj started to attract other forms of outdoor public entertainment, including a music kiosk. From then on, the Bourj began to evolve into an urban hub that encompassed a variety of activities ranging from official state and municipal bureaucracies, travel terminals, hotels, locandas, and sidewalk cafes to retail stores, popular souks, and less reputable venues such as brothels, bars, and gambling houses.

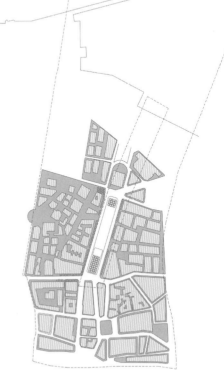

1977 The 1977 APUR plan proposing restoration of the downtown and the softening of the landscape in the Square.

During the Ottoman period (1889–1918), the Bourj underwent successive changes in its popular identity. First it acquired the label of *Sahat al Ittihad* or *al Hamidiyyah,* in reference to its Ottoman legacy—the former as an expression of the desired national unity under Ottoman sovereignty and the latter in commemoration of Sultan Abdul Hamid. By the time Prince Faysal Ibn al-Husayn made his triumphant visit in May 1919, *Sahat al Hamidiyyah* became *Hadiqat al Hurriyah*—freedom from Turkish oppression.

Liberation from Ottoman rule did not of course happen without exacting a heavy toll on leading nationalists. Beginning on August 21, 1915, Jamal Pasha used the open square of the Bourj to hang the first group of eleven. This was followed in 1916 by three other executions (April 5, May 6, and June 5). Journalistic accounts reveal widespread feelings of anguish, trepidation, and pride (see Tueni and Sassine 2000). In 1937, May 6 was declared a national memorial day.

SOLIDERE AND BEIRUT'S HERITAGE AND COLLECTIVE MEMORY

The horrors spawned by the civil war are particularly repugnant because they did nothing to resolve the issues that sparked the hostilities. In this poignant sense, the war that destroyed Beirut was entirely futile. The task of incorporating such events into Beirut's and the country's collective identity is therefore problematic. But it needs to be done; otherwise, the harrowing events might well be trivialized and forgotten, and hence more likely to be repeated.

Since its incorporation on May 5, 1994, the Lebanese Company for Development and Reconstruction of Beirut's central district, known as Solidere, has consolidated itself as the most compelling program of urban reconstruction in Lebanon's history. Some observers go further and herald the venture as one of the largest contemporary urban development projects in the world.

The project covers approximately 1.8 million m² (455 acres); this includes the site of the traditional Bourj district of 1.2 m² (296 acres) along with 159 acres of landfill reclaimed from the sea. Consistent with the project's professed rationale, 225 acres will consist of public space, of which 146 acres are roads and close to 80 acres are public open space. In more explicit terms, this offers a mix of facilities totaling 4.69 million m.² Altogether this amounts to about 8 percent of the surface area of greater metropolitan Beirut.

Solidere's uniqueness is not only a reflection of its scale. The company is more than just a land and real-estate developer. It serves in three other vital capacities: as property owner, manager, and operator. It is entrusted with the responsibility for reconstruction and development of Beirut's Central District (BCD). As stated in Solidere's official memorandum of November 1993, the main features and objectives of the master plan are formidable:

A model of Saifi Village, a "new" residential development around Martyrs Square. (Source: Solidere)

> [creation of] links between "traditional BCD" and reclaimed land; preservation of the historic core of the city between the Serail and Bourj Square; a new financial district mixed with entertainment and shopping facilities on the reclaimed land; reconstruction of the old souks; extension of the residential area to recreate the old distinctive "Levantine city scape"; creation of a seashore park overlooking a new marina near St. George's Bay; extension of Beirut's famous public promenade; integration between BCD and the rest of the city; and limitation of the number of high-rise buildings.

The rationale or philosophy of the master plan is reiterated in Solidere's *Annual Report* of 2000:

The plan respects the main natural features and topography of the site by maximising views of the sea and surrounding landscape; dwells on the formation of public spaces; remains faithful to the urban fabric through preserving and restoring historical urban elements; and ensures the harmonious integration of traditional and modern architecture. It accommodates a broad mix of land uses including business, government, residential, as well as cultural and recreational facilities.

One can easily extract four defining goals that underlie Solidere's scheme: 1) to complement and enrich Beirut's compelling natural habitat; 2) to keep the newly created public spaces faithful to the city's urban fabric by preserving its historical features; 3) to ensure the harmonious integration of traditional and modern architecture; and 4) to accommodate the broadest possible mixture of land uses, including business, government, residential, and recreational and cultural facilities. The overall land-use guidelines of the master plan comply with its avowed objectives of creating a vibrant and cosmopolitan hub with a plurality of activities, yet malleable enough to be adjusted in compliance with changing market conditions

A reconstruction project of this magnitude is bound to invite polemics and heated debate. Critics charge that Solidere has ignored constructive criticism and that the colossal rebuilding has bulldozed much of the legacy of the old city. Dazzling as the emergent city might seem, the wholesale destruction has weakened Beirut's collective memory and alienated many of its traditional inhabitants, critics argue. Even those inclined to overlook Solidere's questionable strategies in appropriating and indemnifying the original real estate holders continue to critique the outcome as a radical rupture with the city's distinct heritage as an open, pluralistic, and cosmopolitan urban center. This rupture, Jad Tabet claims, is a "radical mutation" driven by market forces. It alienates itself from some of the redeeming elements of the city's historic hybrid identity while retaining the prominence of religious edifices—an ominous feature of the belligerent past (*Daily Star,* February 16, 2002: 12).

But one can advance a more measured view of Solidere's record. Beirut sits on an archeological trove of immense symbolic value; everywhere you dig, you are bound to unearth some rare artifact. Solidere's newsletters are replete with reports of wondrous finds, many of which were a surprise to the excava-

Martyrs Square during the Civil War and in the beginning of the clearing for reconstruction.

tors. The monuments, made more visible by the restoration process (along with a substantial number of religious, public, and private institutional buildings) make up the collective memory of the city. So do the commercial landmarks, traditional souks, and labyrinthine residential quarters with their picturesque façades and arcades that symbiotically merge form and function.

Whether Solidere could have preserved more of these features continues to invite debate. Enough has been restored, however, to reclaim the threatened heritage of the city and safeguard its revival. What is most impressive is not only the concern for meeting the technical and aesthetic specifications of each project but the stunning character of the outcome.

There is more to the rehabilitation process than the renewal of façades. Behind the elaborately restored exteriors—the product of exquisite craftsmanship and stonemasonry to highlight the original quality of the old stone in its multiple hues (whether sand, lime, or marble), along with well-crafted wood or iron railings—are completely modernized interiors. The defining elements of the Mediterranean city are rendered more sensitive to the rational demands of contemporary life, leisure, and business.

1991 Dar al-Handasah / Henri Eddeh master plan proposing the Square at the ground axis that leads to the World Trade Center at the harbor.

Through this restorative venture, and perhaps for the first time in recent history, a growing segment of Lebanese are becoming more aware of their spatial surroundings. It has also enhanced public concern for safeguarding their habitat. Citizens are transforming their tenuous attachments to "space" to the more personal and committed loyalties to "place."

THE BOURJ AS PLAYGROUND AND PUBLIC SPHERE

Just as one can understand the resurgence of religious identities in postwar Beirut, one can likewise appreciate the seductive appeal of the Bourj as a playground, an open setting conducive to fluid encounters. Indeed, as we have seen, the Bourj has been adept at accommodating the sacred and the profane, the communal and the associational, the universal and the particular, the global and the local.

This flexibility has rendered the Bourj more able to foster popular culture, mass politics, and, of late, global consumerism, with all its disheartening manifestations of commodification, kitsch, and the debasement of high culture.

Clearly the proliferation of meeting spaces, most visible around the Bourj and adjoining areas, has been conducive to supporting popular culture.

The mandate period saw the emergence of distinctly bourgeois spaces and lifestyles, which led to the formation of a new mass culture. Perquisites of the elite in the late Ottoman period started to spread to middle and lower strata. By the mid-1920s, a new phase of capitalist penetration introduced a multitude of imported consumer goods and practices. As Thompson (2000: 181) indicates, little girls in the mountains of Lebanon were already wearing imported French dresses. By the early 1940s, a set of household inventories showed that average families in Lebanon were enjoying the use of many imported or Western-style products: electric irons, dress shirts, toothbrushes, aspirin, electric lamps, telephones, packaged cookies, canned meat, tuna and sardines, chairs made of iron and wood, and gramophone records.

Electricity did not only make evening events more glamorous; it also expanded the horizons of the urban public with extended tramlines, radios, and telephones. Electricity was introduced to Beirut before World War I. In less than a decade, Beirut had close to 1,000 subscribers. Telephones, long confined to military networks, spread gradually during the 1930s to homes, offices, and public spaces. By 1935, there were phone booths at most busy intersections in Beirut (for these and other details, see Thompson 2000: 180–182).

This intense social mobilization and mass communication was furthered by rapid urbanization throughout the 1950s and 1960s. It was then that Beirut's image as a sophisticated polyglot meeting place of world cultures was being burnished. All indicators attest to this reality: sharp increases in the flow of domestic and foreign mail, and in the number of telephones and passenger vehicles; stupendous growth in the media (particularly television, radio, and movies). All point to appreciable increases in degrees of physical and psychic mobility and high levels of consumption throughout society.

On these and related indices, Lebanon enjoyed higher rates than those observed in adjoining Arab states. Shortly after independence, for example, Lebanon had more than 8,000 passenger vehicles, or about 7 per 1,000 people—considerably more than Syria, Jordan, Iraq, or Egypt in 1960. By then, Lebanon had 73,000,

1996 Revised Dar al-Handasah master plan.

or close to 40 cars per 1,000 people, compared to an average of 4 to 6 among neighboring Arab states (UNESCO 1985, Khalaf 1992). By the early 1920s, Beirut already had three or four cinemas. Unlike in other cities in the Levant, cinemas were not socially and politically contested forms of public entertainment. Cinemas made their first appearance in traditional quarters, sharing makeshift tents with itinerant shadow-puppet shows. Others were temporarily located in the upper floors of cafes, merchant hostels, or locandas. As for other outlets of popular culture, it was the Bourj that became the first permanent space for movie houses. Because of their commodious premises and capacity to accommodate large audiences, cinemas were often used as lecture halls and venues for other cultural events.

If measured by the number of movie seats per capita, Beirut in the 1950s was already reinforcing its reputation as one of the movie capitals of the world. By then, per capita movie attendance was five per year. In another decade, it increased fivefold, making the city a close second to Hong Kong (UNESCO 1965). During the same period, the number of movie theaters leaped from 48 to 170. The accessibility of such theaters, rendered more appealing by the wide variety of films shown, plush surroundings, and low prices, only served to whet the appetite of Lebanese of all classes for this form of public entertainment. Before the advent of television and home videos, anticipating, attending, and talking about movies was the most popular national pastime.

Lebanon was also a nation of journalists. Since the appearance of its first newspaper in 1858, the Lebanese have displayed a talent for establishing newspapers and periodicals that was sustained by a common compulsion for reading them. Families—more than ideological parties, advocacy groups, or political platforms—have provided the motivation for some of the most gifted writers to launch journalistic careers. Fathers served as mentors and role models, initiating sons into the family tradition, honing their skills and cultivating contacts (for further details, see Tueni 1995).

By 1975, on the eve of the civil war, Lebanon had more than 400 publication licenses. For a country of about 3 million, this is an incredible density of newsprint. The majority of newspapers were politically independent, though a small number might be associated with a particular political group.

Economic and social historians are keen on attributing Beirut's cosmopolitanism and tolerance of foreign cultures to its mercantile predisposition. The exchange of goods and services rests, after all, on the willingness to interact with others. Throughout its history, Beirut has lived up to its image as being part of a merchant republic. The Bourj, in particular, served as a magnet for banks, credit houses, and exchange outlets. Charles Issawi describes the scene:

> Fabulous, yet perfectly authentic, stories are told of the transfer of gold from Mexico to India and China, of the shipment of copper from Franco's Spain to Stalin's Russia and of the sale of a huge consignment of toothbrushes from an Italian firm to a neighboring one—and all directed from and financed by some mangy-looking business house in Beirut. In 1951, when Lebanon's gold trade was at its peak, it was estimated that 30 percent of world gold traffic passed thorough the country. (Issawi 1966: 284)

As in virtually all other commercial and industrial enterprises, many of the early banking and financial houses were family establishments. Kinship, however, was not a source of harmful nepotism. Rather, family pride acted as a spur for inventiveness and fierce competition.

Beirut's ebullient cosmopolitanism at times made the city (and especially the Bourj) vulnerable to the vicissitudes of internal and regional disturbances; it became open to abuse by the very forces that sought it as a haven from repression or homelessness. A free press, absence of exchange controls, secret bank accounts, liberal migration laws, receptivity to novelties and fads, tolerance of progressive and permissive lifestyles—all reinforce the discordant dualism inherent it Beirut's character as a free and open city. All too often, Beirut became no more than an expedient conduit, a transit point, for the trafficking and recycling of displaced groups, goods, capital, and ideas.

The city (like much of the rest of the country) became notorious for smuggling, arms-running, trading in drugs, black-marketing of contraband, and other illegal activities. Dissident groups exploited media freedom to launch vilifying press campaigns against repressive regimes in the region, which provoked retribution by the targeted states or groups against Lebanon.

As a metaphor, a "playground" conjures up images of an open, accommodating space, for inventiveness and experimentation, but also a site of excessive passions and indulgent egoism. In this sense, it is a more neutral metaphor than the hackneyed labels of Beirut as a wondrous and privileged creation, as a "Switzerland" or "Paris" of the Middle East; or worse, the more pejorative tags with which it has been maligned lately. A more inclusive metaphor, it allows us to illuminate certain inescapable realities.

A "playground" is more than just a heuristic and analytical tool; it also has cathartic and redemptive features. By eliciting those latent longings for play, conviviality, and adventure, a "playground" may well serve as an expressive and transcending outlet. It brings out all the "Homo Ludens" virtues of fair play, the exuberance of individual and competitive sports, and rewards for feats of excellence. In this respect, a "playground" becomes an ideal site for cultivating the virtues of civility and commitment to the rules of the game. The very survival of a playground, particularly since it is associated with spaces where children can indulge in play, is predicated on the premise of monitoring and controlling the hazards of reckless impulse. When uncontained, a "playground" could easily slip into a free-for-all—a raucous, rough-and-tumble public ground. It is then that lines demarcating civil and uncivil acts, couth and uncouth behavior, foul and fair play, are blurred. Indeed, fair sometimes becomes foul, and foul fair.

The curative and healing aspects of a playground are naturally more pertinent in times of collective unrest and postwar stress and uncertainty. A boisterous political culture suffused with factional rivalries can find more than just momentary release in such outlets. Some of the enabling features of a playground—fair play, teamwork, equal recognition, and the sheer exuberance of doing one's thing without encroaching on the rights and spaces of others—can all aid in the restoration of civility. At least they need not be dismissed and trivialized.

Inordinate resources have been squandered on strategies of political and administrative reform and the broader issues of regional conflict and infrastructural reconstruction. Important as these are, they overlook some of the more human and sociocultural issues of coping with pervasive fear and damaged national identities. It is these areas that are amenable to individual intervention. Ordinary citizens are given opportunities to participate and become actively and meaningfully engaged in processes of reconstruction and rehabilitation. The Bourj as an open public sphere could very well become such an engaging and spirited place.

FUTURE PROSPECTS

This is a critical watershed in Beirut's history. Once again, the city center is in the throes of reinventing itself. No other space in Lebanon is as ideally situated to serve as an open and engaging public sphere than the Bourj. This ability of Beirutis to adapt to new settings and to experiment with hybrid and cosmopolitan lifestyles must be safeguarded.

The challenge of urban planning and design is to consider strategies through which the redemptive, healing, and enabling features of a common public sphere (or playground) can be nurtured while safeguarding the Bourj from slipping into a dystopia of a fashionable resort or a zone within which competing confessional communities assert their public identities. The Bourj has always been able to preserve some of its local traditions despite the incessant transformations it had to accommodate. It is this receptivity to cross-cultural contacts that accounts for its survival as a cosmopolitan public sphere.

The politics of civil society, as John Keane (2001), John Friedman (1994), and Iris Young (1990), among others, insist on reminding us, is emancipatory in at least two vital senses. First, they enlarge the sphere of autonomy, particularly by providing public spaces based on trust, reciprocity, and dialogue. Second, they provide venues for the mobilization of multiple voices and hence political empowerment. Young here makes a useful distinction between autonomy, which is largely the sphere of the private, where groups can make decisions that affect primarily their own welfare without interference by others, and political empowerment, which calls for effective participation in all decisions that affect the public welfare (Young 1990: 250–252).

Both are particularly relevant strategies at this critical watershed in Lebanon's history, when the nation is caught between the throes of postwar rehabilitation and the disquieting manifestations of global and postmodern transformations. The promise of autonomy remains inherent in this ability to encourage the active engagement and self-management of the myriad local voluntary associations that have mushroomed during the past decade. Among other things, this calls for a dissenting and oppositional politics and the provision of venues for cultural resistance. Political empowerment, on the other hand, implies a shift from the essentially private and parochial concerns of civil society to the sphere of political community. Here politics become a struggle for inclusion, an opportunity for self-actualization and a form of social justice that acknowledges the needs and priorities of different groups.

There is also another sense through which the concern for autonomy and empowerment can be particularly redemptive in Lebanon. Given regional and global constraints, it is understandable that Lebanon might not be able to safeguard its national sovereignty or contain some of the global forces that undermine its political independence and economic well-being. At the sociocultural and psychic levels, however, the opportunities to participate in such voluntary outlets can do much to nurture some of the civil virtues that will reinforce prospects for greater measures of autonomy and empowerment.

Postwar interludes, particularly those coming in the wake of prolonged periods of civil disorder, anarchy, and reckless bloodletting, normally generate moods of restraints, disengagement, and moderation. War-weary people typically are inclined to curb their ordinary impulses and become more self-controlled in the interest of reassessing the legacy of their belligerent past and redefining their future options. Somehow, postwar Lebanon has produced the opposite reactions. Rather than releasing the Lebanese from their prewar excesses, the times have unleashed appetites and inflamed people with insatiable desires for extravagant consumerism, acquisitiveness, and longing for immoderate forms of leisure and sterile recreative outlets. Some of the dismaying byproducts of such mindless excesses, particularly those that continue to defile the country's habitat and living spaces, have become more egregious. Here as well, the active engagement in the burgeoning voluntary sector can be effective in resisting the forces of excessive commodification, government dysfunction, and corruption.

Concerted efforts must be made in this regard to redirect the obsessive interest of the Lebanese in the hedonistic and ephemeral pleasures of consumerism to more productive and resourceful outlets. Consumption is essentially a passive preoccupation when compared to the more productive and creative pursuits of doing things for oneself in association with others, which should not be underestimated as a source of collective healing and rejuvenation. All productive activities, as John Friedman (1998:33–35) reminds us, are inherently cooperative. Hence active engagement in a medley of activities—sports, music, neighborhood improvement, social welfare, human rights promotion, education programs, participation in advocacy groups on behalf of the excluded and marginalized, and above all, cultural and artistic pursuits—are all potentially transformative experiences.

By transforming the private concerns of autonomy into sites of political empowerment, where issues of public concern are debated and addressed, such venues will also become the most redemptive settings for the cultivation of civil virtues. It is in such hybrid and open spaces that this cultivation of civility will allow groups to appreciate their differences without being indifferent to others. The Bourj is poised to reclaim its legacy.

References

Davie, May. 2003. "Beirut and the Étoile Area: An Exclusively French Project." In Joe Nasr and M. Volait, eds., *Urbanism: Imported or Exported*. New York: Wiley-Academy, 206–229.

Friedman, J. 1994. *Cultural Identity and Global Process*. London: Sage.

Gavin, A. 1998. "Heart of Beirut: Making the Master Plan for the Renewal of the Central District." In Peter Rowe and Hashim Sarkis, eds., *Projecting Beirut*. Munich: Prestel, 217–234.

Illich, Ivan. 1980. *The Tools of Conviviality*. New York: Harper and Row.

Issawi, Charles. 1966. "Economic Development and Political Liberalism in Lebanon." In L. Binder, ed., *Politics in Lebanon*. New York: Wiley, 69–83.

Jessup, Henry, H. 1910. *Fifty-three Years in Syria*. New York: Fleming Revell.

Keane, John. 2001. *Civil Society: Old Images and New Visions*. New York: Oxford and Stanford.

Khalaf, Samir. 1985. "Social Structure and Urban Planning in Lebanon." In Ann Elizabeth Mayer, ed., *Property, Social Structure, and Law in the Modern Middle East*. New York: SUNY, 213–235.

Khalaf, Samir. 1993. "Urban Design and the Recovery of Beirut." In Samir Khalaf and Philip Khoury, eds., *Recovering Beirut*. Leiden: E.J. Brill, 11–60.

Mathur, A. 1999. "Neither Wilderness, Nor Home: The Indian Maidan." In James Corner, ed., *Recovering Landscapes*. New York: Princeton Architecture Press, 205–219.

Nasr, Salim. 1978. "The Crisis of Lebanese Capitalism." *MERIP Reports*. December, No. 73, 3–13.

Neale, F.A. 1952. *Eight Years in Syria, Palestine, and Asia Minor*, vol. 1 (second edition). London: Colburn.

Nussbaum, M.C. 1997. "Kant and Cosmopolitanism." In Bohman and Lutz Bachman, eds., *Perpetual Peace*. Cambridge, MA: MIT Press, 25–57.

Salam, Assem. 1993. "Lebanon's Experience with Urban Planning: Problems and Prospects." In Khalaf and Khoury, eds., *Recovering Beirut*, 194–201.

Salam, Assem. 1998. "The Role of Government in Shaping the Built Environment." In Rowe and Sarkis, eds., *Projecting Beirut*, 122–134.

Sarkis, Hashim. 1998. "Dances with Margaret Mead: Planning Beirut since 1958." In Rowe and Sarkis, eds., *Projecting Beirut*, 187–201.

Sarkis, Hashim. 2004. *Circa 1958*. Beirut: Dar An-Nahar.

Solidere. 2000. *Annual Report*. Beirut: Solidere.

Stanhope, Lady Hester. 1846. *Memoirs of the Lady Hester Stanhope*, vol. 1 (second edition). London: Henry Colburn.

Thompson, Elizabeth. 2000. *Colonial Citizens*. New York: Columbia University Press.

Tueni, G. 1995. *Sirr al Mehnah Wa Asrar Qukhra* (Professional Secrets and Others). Beirut: Dar An-Nahar.

Tueni, G., and F. Sassine, eds. 2000. *El Bourj: Place de la Liberté et Porte du Levant*. Beirut: Dar An-Nahar.

UNESCO. 1985. *UNESCO Statistical Yearbook*.

Young, I.M. 1990. *Justice and the Politics of Difference*. Princeton, NJ: Princeton University Press.

CONSIDERING PUBLIC LIFE IN BEIRUT

MARK DWYER

Contemporary cities are increasingly evaluating their urban performance to determine how they can compete in the global economy. With each new urban project, new models of development are explored and old models challenged. This reconsideration of contemporary city making has brought about a greater concern for the viability of the city than in previous generations, most visibly in recent periodicals and project competitions. Urbanist Joan Busquets explains that "in the case of Urbanism and Urban Architecture, this act of reconsideration seems particularly necessary: firstly, we get the feeling that the paradigms which directed the actions and plans of the XXth century are no longer relevant or have been played out, and secondly, the city and the projects based on it have a much higher-profile presence than ever before."[1] Regenerating the city will demand new lines of urban interventions specific to the needs of the contemporary city and geared toward the definition and creation of a desired public life, encouraged by clear public policy.

Arguably, Beirut is one of the best examples of a city working to evaluate its urban future. Faced with the postwar reconstruction of its ancient city center, and after a slow and often tumultuous start to its rebuilding, Beirut may still have a great chance to develop a completely new public life for itself. The

01 Vacant parcels along Martyrs Square. (All images in this chapter courtesy of author, unless otherwise noted)

emptiness left by the postwar clearing of the downtown has allowed for a wide array of urban design scenarios to be imagined for its reconstruction. Unfortunately, the progress to date has offered little reassurance that this new public life will ever emerge. A continued preference for the automobile and the role of public space as development incentive has left both urban life and the pedestrian out of the current debate.

As the competition to determine the future of Beirut's most symbolic urban space, Martyrs Square, comes to the attention of the international design community, the fate of public life in Beirut may rest on its outcome. With so much at stake, the realization of this entirely new future remains to be determined by Solidere, the Lebanese company charged with the reconstruction and development of Beirut's central district (BCD), and its willingness to equate urban life with urban development. This essay will look at the absence of a defined urban-space policy for Beirut within the context of more established precedents of good city form in an attempt to position the challenge of rebuilding an old city center with a new urban life.

CONTEXT To begin a discussion of Beirut's public-space policies, it is necessary to take stock of the current situation of the city and its most recent history. Beginning in the middle of the last century, many urbanized areas suffered greatly from heavy investment in automobiles and the associated infrastructure that dominated urban development. Beirut was no exception. Cities became congested, urban quality deteriorated, and open space became parking space, discouraging social interaction and encouraging an even greater retreat from the center. The fear of losing what Jan Gehl refers to as meeting places and market-places—and leaving only traffic spaces—forced many cities to propose bold new public-space policies.[2]

As other cities began to address their urban cores, Beirut began a fifteen-year civil war in 1975, which essentially froze its attitude toward urban space and automobiles in the early 1970s. Although Beirut's traffic problems, as they relate to pedestrians and tourism, are still quite serious, they are not the defining feature of the city. Beirut offers several obvious amenities that would be the envy of most urbanized areas. Its Mediterranean coastline, ancient historical sites, scenic mountain ranges, and diverse multilingual population make it an attractive context in which to live or visit.

The unfortunate devastation and emptiness left by the civil war has afforded the city the opportunity to rethink and rebuild its traditionally congested urban core. The current reconstruction of Beirut is under the guidance of a master plan, administered by Solidere and built through both public and private investment. Much of its effort has been focused on infrastructure and technology, making the central business district both highly modern and practically viable. Substantially less time has been given to public spaces and the everyday urbanism associated with the people who live in metropolitan Beirut. In Solidere's defense, it has provided for Beirut what citizens typically demand of their municipalities but seldom receive: completed portions of the city boast clean streets, sufficient infrastructure, and secure places to interact. The best example, the Etoile, is a successful pedestrian area that caters mainly to international shopping and expensive French-style cafes. The Etoile is often criticized, however, for its high maintenance, high commercial rental rates, and the heavy control of street vendors, who often ques-

02 Cafe style seating in the Etoile area

tion who the reconstruction is for. In its decade of existence, Solidere has worked hard for the reconstruction, but the city is less than half rebuilt and many tough decisions lay ahead.

BEIRUT'S PUBLIC SPACES

The need for a new counterproject in Beirut is more apparent than ever, based on the general sense of disinterest the public has shown for recent spaces created in the downtown. Solidere's "greening" of the master plan has left much to be desired in terms of effective public spaces. Treatment of public space in the master plan is typically keyed as "green open space" with the standard "parking below" designation—and no other distinctions as to form or program. The most finished of these spaces have confirmed Solidere's lack of position toward defining the civic life of Beirut. Khalil Gibran Garden, Riad El Solh Square, and the recently completed Debbas Square all reveal the inadequacy of the plan. In each case, the existing or proposed programs that front onto the squares give little reference to the forms or activities of the squares themselves or to their differing locations within the central business district. Gibran Garden, at the southern face of Pierre El Khoury's United Nations building, acts more as a buffer to the elevated highway than an urban gesture to the city. Its formal emptiness, surrounded on three sides by high-speed infrastructure, creates a backyard island condition to the UN building and the downtown. The Square's awkward placement on the periphery of the core, wedged between the very nonpublic, guarded program of the United Nations and the 1960s elevated highway, gives it little hope of ever adding to the public life of the city.

Nearby Riad El Solh Square does little more than widen the sidewalk and change the paving to signify this historically significant clearing outside the old city walls. Arriving at the Square on foot proves too challenging for so little reward, as pedestrians confront one of the most congested and topographically awkward traffic intersections in the downtown. For the moment, Riad El Solh merely buffers a large surface parking lot from the intersection with dense vegetation and a mounded earth base. The Square is intended to front the future site of Jean Nouvel's long-anticipated Landmark project (now the parking lot). Nouvel's large mixed-use project and tower will inevitably alter the Square's identity and program, but its place and effectiveness in the city is still to be determined.

03 Gibran Garden looking towards the elevated highway

04 View of Gibran Garden, between the elevated highway and the central business district

05 View of Riad El Solh Statue and the landscape buffer

06 Future site of Jean Nouvel's Landmark Center adjacent to Riad El Solh Square

The newest addition to public space in Beirut is Debbas Square in Saifi. This full-block space, surrounded by streets on all sides, may be more overly designed than some of the new architecture in the BCD. Although it is close to Martyrs Square, this space seems situated more for the growing high-end residential neighborhood of Saifi than for the public realm of Beirut. There is also missed potential for connections to the Etoile, Martyrs Square, or the nearby nightclubs of Rue Monot in Ashrafieh. In terms of urban design, the space lacks orientation in the city, flexibility of use, and simplicity of plan, and features a large blue wall that overwhelms the diminutive square and surrounding area. Although the Square is most closely associated with Saifi Village, it still isn't clear exactly who or what this space is for. The Debbas example best illustrates the use of public space within Solidere as an urban "carrot," used mainly to attract developers to build projects along its adjacent vacant parcels.

This open-space treatment by the city may ultimately be the fate of all other spaces in the BCD if new development and investment in the downtown continue at a slow pace. One such example at risk would be the green parcel for Wadi Abou Jamil, which has the potential to be a key centralized community space for this mostly residential district. The site offers several dynamic urban features; it is well positioned at the base of the Grand Serail hill along one of the visual axes of the master plan, and it is adjacent to Beirut's only synagogue. If situated within a more defined urban-space strategy, it could create one of the best places for local urban life in the future fabric of the downtown. The site in Wadi Abou Jamil shares the condition of Debbas Square in that vacant parcels, awaiting development, surround its edges and leave its future in doubt. These same concerns can be raised for the futures of Ajami Square, Khan Antoun Bey Square, and Bab Santiyyeh along the historic harbor walk.

If these new spaces are considered alongside Beirut's most successful urban space, the Corniche, the differences are dramatic. The Corniche is certainly privileged by its adjacency to the Mediterranean, but its modest surfaces, dimensions, and vegetation should provide clues for developing other spaces in the city. The Corniche is neither expensively paved nor intensely planted, yet it draws thousands of people from very early in the morning to late at night: locals mingle, children swim, and everyone enjoys walking along the sea and watching other people. The Corniche provides space for individuals and groups, is highly accessible by car (a must in Beirut), welcomes street vendors and musicians, has abundant places to sit, and most of all, is always "open." The Corniche model is key to returning public life to the people of Beirut.

PRECEDENTS Although the public-space policy for Beirut should emerge from local conditions specific to the region, planners should not feel the need to create entirely new models for constructing the city. Beirut can draw inspiration from various international precedents that nonetheless respond to the particular needs of its urban environment. In the tradition of Beirut's historic reliance on European planning, two European examples of public-space policy can help provide clues for the reconstruction: Copenhagen, for its incremental pro-pedestrian policies in the city, and Rotterdam, for its postwar/post-industrial reconstruction strategies. Both of these cities have established and continue to thrive on clear public-space polices that consider the city in its entirety.

07 "Blue Wall" in Debbas Square, Saifi Village

COPENHAGEN Copenhagen began its urban-space policies earlier than most cities, in 1962, with the conversion of a major street in the inner city to exclusively pedestrian use. Copenhagen in the 1960s, much like Beirut today, had little tradition of outdoor public life and even less of public-space design. What it did have was a dense urban center completely dominated by car traffic and parking. The city decided that through the incremental addition of street conversions to pedestrian use, a network of safe public spaces would eventually result. In addition to its growing pedestrian network, many new squares of varied recreational uses were introduced, most converted from parking lots. These new squares created a variety of breathing spaces along the expanding pedestrian routes through the city.

Over the next several decades, as the difficulty and expense of driving and parking in the city increased, so too did the consideration of alternatives such as public transit, cycling, and walking. To free spaces for new city life, parking in the inner city was reduced by 2–3 percent annually. Motorists gradually grew accustomed to paying more to park or to leaving their cars at home.[3] Over the past forty years, Copenhagen has reclaimed not only its commercial center for pedestrians but much of its natural amenities as well.

Several parallels can be drawn between the urban scenarios of Beirut and those of Copenhagen from decades past; neither possessed a real sense of public life, and both downtowns were overwhelmed by automobiles. Early elements of Beirut's reconstruction, however, continue to give preference to cars. One of Beirut's initial projects involved the widening of many key streets in the city center and proportionally reducing sidewalk widths and uses, essentially encouraging additional traffic. Although the Etoile exists as a pedestrian-friendly zone in Beirut, it is more the result of securing the elite in the downtown and less the foundation of pedestrian network logic for the city. This attitude toward urban design may ultimately threaten much of Beirut's potential growth as a city of tourism, as future visitors from the west may prefer to experience the city on foot than through the window of a car.

ROTTERDAM The case of Rotterdam differs significantly from that of Copenhagen, as the Dutch have a long tradition of pedestrian life coupled with a reliance on bicycles, but it may provide other clues for Beirutis. Rotterdam sustained heavy bombardment during World War II, and the eventual shifting of its port out of the inner city permitted both a postwar and a post-industrial reconsideration to occur. City planners viewed Rotterdam as containing four distinct areas, each with its own specific characteristics. While the boundaries of these areas were blurred and sometimes overlapped, they remained strongly connected through large urban structuring devices. The cultural route, the city axis, and railroad tunnel route all positioned the individual districts of the downtown within a larger context and added coherence.[4]

The attractiveness of today's inner city is determined by opportunities for personal encounters and the exchange of ideas; it is born of a density of cultural activities, amusement, and recreation. Rotterdam's public-space policy has provided many excellent examples of contemporary urban-space design.

Among them undoubtedly are the commercially successful Lijnbaan, Schouwburgplein (plaza) designed by West 8, and the still developing Kop Van Zuid district (the once industrial waterfront along the Maas). Although Rotterdam has maintained its position as the world's largest commercial seaport, it now also offers a strong sense of public life with dynamic urban spaces. Rotterdam does not claim to compete with traditional European standards for the scenic or historic, but it does offer a condition more aligned with the development of other contemporary cities—mainly in its conversion of former industrial sites along its waterfront to residential uses and its reliance on commercial centers for economic stability.

Beirut's central district is well placed for a similar treatment to that of Rotterdam. If the different districts of the downtown are considered as having unique characteristics and designed to reflect those differences, a strategy emerges for the entire city. The current master plan has provided a guide for the different parts of the downtown: the hotel district and marina, Wadi Abou Jamil, the Serail Hill, Etoile, Saifi, Martyrs Square, and the international waterfront district can all be considered parts of the whole. These districts can be brought together by the larger systems of the city: the archeological trail, the Corniche, the master axes, and so on. This logic would allow for new urban spaces to not only fulfill the "green" requirements of the master plan but also cultivate an urban life more reflective of the city and how people use it.

Notes
1. Joan Busquets, *"Urbanism at the turn of the century,"* The Fifth Van Eesteren/Van Lohuizen lecture, Amsterdam, 2000.
2. Jan Gehl and Lars Gemzoe, *"New City Spaces,"* third edition (Copenhagen: Danish Architectural Press, 2003). See also Gehl and Gemzøe, *"Public Space, Public Life: Copenhagen 1996"* (Copenhagen: Danish Architectural Press and the Royal Danish Academy of Fine Arts, School of Architecture, 1996).
3. Ibid.
4. Johan Goossens, Anja Guinee, and Wiebe Oosterhoff, eds., *"Public Space: Design, Layout, and Management of Public Space in Rotterdam"* (Rotterdam: 010 Publishers, 1995).

The projects focus on the redesign of Martyrs Square, Beirut's primary public square before the war and the center of many contested views about public life, urban development, and the interface between new development and architectural and archeological heritage. The participants in the studio were twelve students from the three design programs at the GSD: architecture, urban design, and landscape architecture. This diversity in background of the studio participants enriched the discussion and supported the desire to seek creative synthesis of the various attributes of a public square.

The studio was conducted in collaboration with Solidere, the real estate holding company in charge of the redevelopment of downtown Beirut. This study took place as the company's town-planning group was preparing for an international competition held around the Square. The timing helped us significantly in entering the debate, albeit in a broader, more pedagogical, and less strictly structured way than the competition brief would demand. Yet the competition helped situate the projects in response to some of the contemporary factors that are shaping the city's architectural and urban culture. We hope that these projects can be viewed as an extension of a more focused debate generated by the parallel ideas competition organized by Solidere and the Union of International Architects in 2004–2005, which included participation by many of the students (and awards for Aaron Cohen and Claudia Mejia).

More than ten years after embarking on a major reconstruction project, the city of Beirut is still looking for a clear strategy for Martyrs Square, its primary public square. Although the reconstruction master plan does indicate the re-creation of several open spaces, as argued by Mark Dwyer in his essay, very few of these have

SQUARE ONE STUDIO:
SITE AND CONTEXT

been designed or built in a convincing manner. The adopted master plan tends to define open spaces by deferring their character to the surrounding buildings, thus reinforcing the strategy that buildings, not roads or open spaces, define the character of the city. Given the scale of the Square and the vast clearing around it, this problem is most glaring in the area of Martyrs Square. In launching this competition, Beirut seemed to acknowledge this problem. In more ways than one, the city is going back to square one.

The reconstruction of downtown continues to be a platform on which contending claims over urban life are played out, even if the process of reconstruction has eliminated many of the old players. In the absence of an open political arena, these claims tend to revive political discourse, even if they are made on grounds of aesthetics or good urban development. It is not surprising that the design of Martyrs Square would capture the attention of the general public and professionals alike. It is also not surprising that after the assassination of Rafik Hariri, the former prime minister of Lebanon, his burial and related mass demonstrations, public sit-ins, and concerts would all converge on the contested and charged grounds of Martyrs Square.

The history of the Square, its social life and planning, are well documented in my essay and the chapter by Samir Khalaf. However, it is important to note a few main points here. Once the downtown was cleared for redevelopment in the mid-1990s, the debate over how to rebuild it shifted from deciding on the scale and financial mechanisms to determining degrees of restoration of the center. The plans prepared by Dar al-Handasah, a large corporate design firm, and ratified by the Lebanese parliament for implementation by Solidere, were supposed to be final, but they tended to emphasize regulation over form. They also deferred many key decisions to individual developers and left it up to them to negotiate their way with Solidere, the supervisor of the plan's execution. Even matters of historic preservation, which appeared at first to be clear and straightforward, were open for such negotiations.

Before addressing the design problem, the students studied the history of the Square and the history and current plans for the city center's other squares. Despite the primacy of Martyrs Square, the city center of Beirut holds several public spaces that have been recreated or created from scratch in the reconstruction plan. The aim of this assignment was to better understand the nature of these spaces and assess how to define them to enhance their particularities while upholding the primacy of Martyrs Square. Some of these analyses, as confirmed in the essay by Mark Dwyer, attest to the fact that the design of public space in Beirut's city center would benefit greatly from the study of the unsuccessful translation of current policies into the design of new public spaces. It would also benefit from exploring the possibilities that a more emphatic urban design approach could bring to the city.

DAVID CUTLER	62
CLAUDIA MEJIA	66
HAMAD AL-EISA	68
SHANNON BASSETT	72
ABBY FELDMAN	74
AARON COHEN	78
REEM ALISSA	82
DAVID FLETCHER	84
ANNA-MARIA BULSKA	86
SAMUEL OLBEKSON	88
YUTAKA SHO	90

SQUARE ONE STUDIO: STUDENT WORK

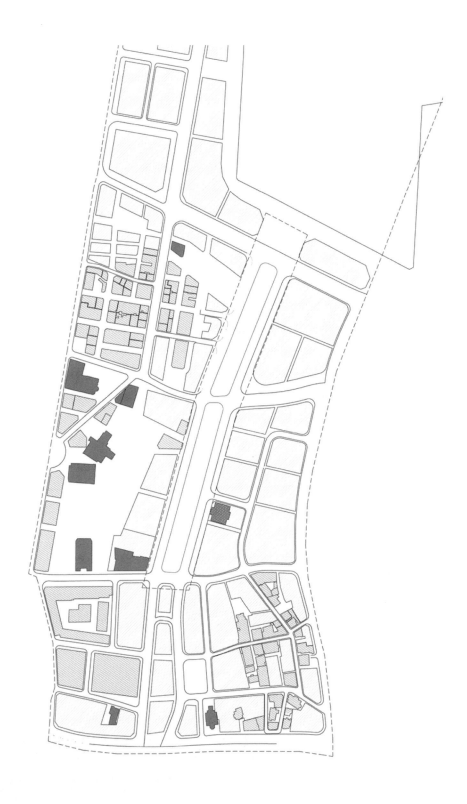

Beirut suffers from collective schizophrenia. Master planners and politicians speculate about an emerging global metropolis, propelled by tremendous infusions of foreign capital. The citizenry envision a cultural center, embodied with the specific histories, traditions, and aspirations of the people. Although neither view is axiomatically exclusive, if current economic and planning mechanisms persist, it is likely that such local and global ideologies will never coexist, even in the most progressive and dynamic of the Arab states.

At the core of the conundrum is the fragility of Lebanon's market. The country's public debt is among the highest in the world, approaching 200 percent of GDP. Interest rates are in the double digits. And with more than 70 percent of the economy operating in U.S. dollars, the government is largely powerless to influence the value of its own currency. The situation reinforces international banks' conservative lending policies, which cripples local businesses and perpetuates the downward financial spiral. Most Beirutis can no longer afford their city, and the government is in no position to help.

Like many reemerging cities, Beirut has encouraged international investment in the hope of filling this void. But Beirut is unique in that it is offering its very identity in return. Solidere, the publicly mandated, privately held real estate company overseeing reconstruction, has offered for sale an area equal to 8 percent of the total land area of the city located at its unquestioned physical, perceptual, and historical center. Demand is high among regional investors, pricing out those Lebanese who once called the area home. In the case of Martyrs Square, marketing and parcelization strategies targeted at foreigners threaten to redistribute the majority stake in a national identity. This proposal repositions Solidere's master plan to allow Beirut's local constituencies an opportunity to buy into the country's most cherished

DAVID CUTLER

real estate, while allowing the flexibility for better-capitalized regional players to continue to invest at a scale commensurate with the pace of global development.

As a starting point, this proposal systematically divides Solidere's grand axis to the sea into spheres of influence based on prevailing patterns of traffic and inter-neighborhood connectivities. Each "sphere" is anchored by a functional public icon and platted to encourage development that differentiates it in scale and scope from its counterparts, but that also allows it the flexibility to expand and contract with the natural fluctuations of adjacent areas and of economic markets. The incessant north-south linearity of the grand axis is diluted by increasing the intensity of plat frontages along each "sphere's" east-west arterial, allowing urbanism to help bridge an axis that many regard as a bitter social divide.

Immediately surrounding Martyrs Square, platting is atomized far beyond that stipulated in Solidere's master plan. (The number of buildable square meters is retained by moving high-rise projects to the harbor edge.) Smaller parcel sizes and building envelopes increase the intensity of street activity and decrease land costs, contributing to the vitality of the Square while allowing entities such as Eagle One, Lebanon's only real estate investment company, or other local interests to hold a real stake in the country's evolving identity and contribute iteratively to the stabilization of the Lebanese economy. Fully public streets replace the percentage of land that had been reserved for private open space within parcels and delineate the distribution of new ground- floor programs. Above the street level, buildings may link to create larger parcels, which, when fully realized over adjacent blocks, define urban courtyards with intersecting streets at their center, rendering public the traditionally private portions of urban life. In the area around the Square, the essential compo-

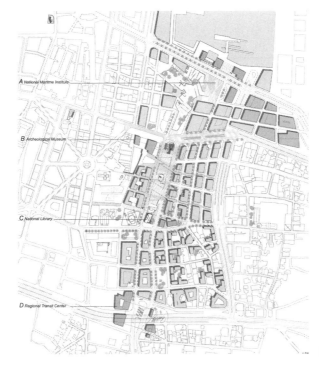

02

01 Perspective toward Martyrs Square with National Library in the center
02 Project site plan showing four "spheres," each anchored by a public icon

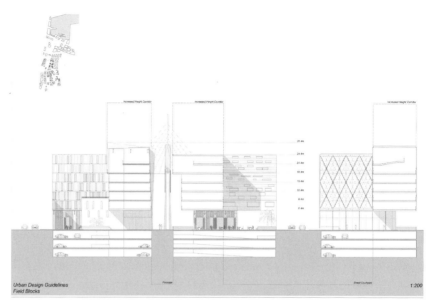

03

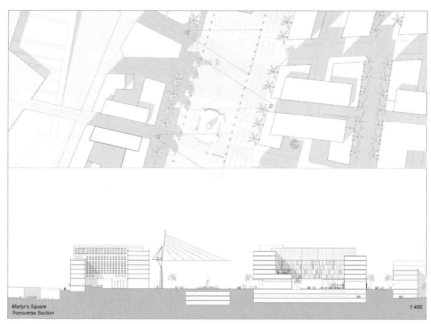

04

03 Martyrs Square: Longitudinal Section
04 Martyrs Square: Transverse Section
05 Urban Design Guidelines: Field Blocks

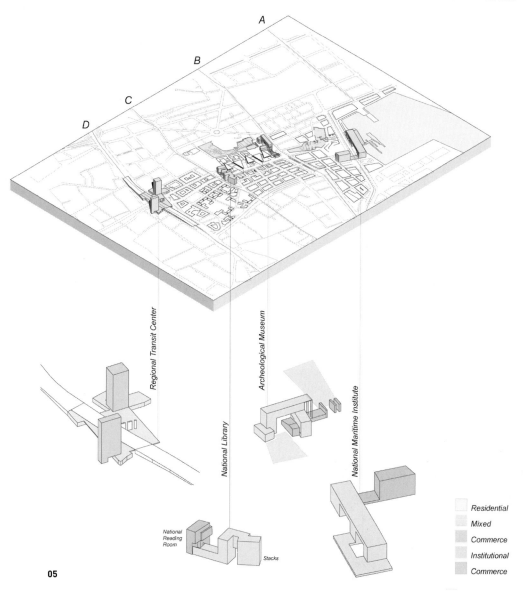

A

B

C

D

Regional Transit Center

Archeological Museum

National Library

National Maritime Institute

National Reading Room

Stacks

Residential

Mixed

Commerce

Institutional

Commerce

05

nents of urbanism are disaggregated from the modern paradigm of the all-in-one building, made smaller, multiplied, and recombined to create a field condition where the public and public-ness are everywhere. The heart of Beirut is once again made available to Beirutis.

Martyrs Square is retained as a void in the patterns created by these "field" neighborhoods and anchoring institutions, owned only by the public and programmed by the fluctuations in circulation systems and market-driven changes in the intensity of adjacent land uses. A mechanized velabrum creates paths of shadow that reach across the Square, changing alignments with the movement of the sun.

01

The first idea of the project is to rethink the proportions of the proposed square and its borders. To position the relevance of Solidere's proposition for the Square, a study was made of its historic perimeters at various key points over time. The form of the Square and the space to the sea had changed through history. The new proposal looks to redefine the borders by taking distinctive elements of the perimeter over the Square's long history, to reestablish the proportions of the site and address its memory. The proposed square resulted into two separated spaces, continuous at the pedestrian level. The area to the north, contained within the archeological site, is proposed as an archeological park, and to the south, the historic Martyrs Square returns as a truly urban public space.

The second idea is to give life back to the Square through the introduction of public buildings. The historical significance of the Square was given by its public character as center of political activities, entertainment, and transportation. The proposed public structures will provide an incentive for the Square to be used. They will attract users of different religions and social strata, making the Square a place of meeting for the whole city. The new public buildings are strategically located in the Square. The national library and the cinema are in the north and south of the Square, enclosing and giving proportion to the space. These buildings provide large canopies that promote the visual and pedestrian continuity of the space. The public buildings complex is also composed by the national theater and the market proposed on the west and east sides of the Square and is complemented by the mosque being built.

The third idea is the reinforcement of the public character of the Square and public buildings through the treatment of surfaces. The horizontal surface of the Square is characterized by folding in different areas, defining openings for parking and other functions. This folding creates enclosed spaces on the pedestrian level and protects those on foot

02

CLAUDIA MEJIA

from auto traffic. The horizontal surface is expanded under public buildings elevated on pilotis, adding new public open spaces.

The definition of the horizontal surfaces ends on the private buildings. In these cases, the project proposes more general vertical surfaces defined by a perimeter that determines the setbacks and arcades that the new private buildings should follow. These perimeters respond to lines present in the historical analysis.

The streets of the Square are also modified, diminishing Solidere's proposed width; this change facilitates pedestrian circulation between the borders of the Square, as defined by the new public and private structures.

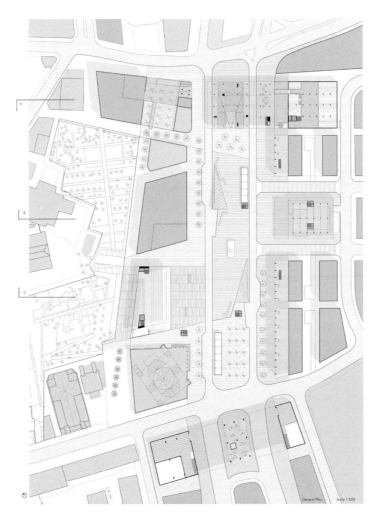

03

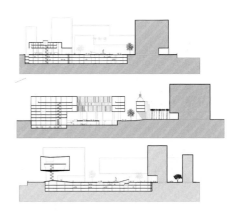

04

01 Martyrs Square: Perspective from North looking through National Library
02 Martyrs Square: Model Photograph from North
03 Martyrs Square: Surface Level Plan
04 Martyrs Square: Transverse Sections

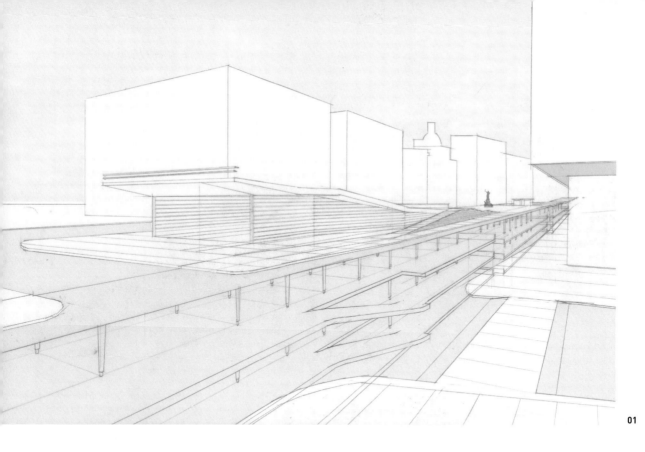

The boundary of the Beirut Central District (BCD) is defined by the highway to the south, major roadways at the east and west, and the sea to the north. Martyrs Square is on the eastern periphery of the BCD, in contrast with its historically central location in Beirut. To reactivate the Square, its central location must be reclaimed. By extending the built fabric to the east of the BCD over George Haddad Street, Martyrs Square shifts from peripheral back to central.

Along Martyrs Square's north-south axis, topography plays a role in the fragmentation of the Square into subsquares that respond to the local program at their respective locations. The 8-meter elevation is negotiated with three flat zones. The first is to the south at the newly proposed bus terminal, creating an infrastructural node of activity. The second zone is at the center of the Square and contains the statue of the martyrs, and is aligned with the old police station, which is to be converted into a national library. The third flat zone is at the south end of the Square at Weygand Street, creating an entry into the proposed underground archeological museum while extending pedestrian networks across the Square into the newly proposed fabric to the east of the Square. Each of these zones is programmed with pedestrian entry points into the underground parking structure. These entry points are articulated with light wells that extend down into the structure.

The transitions between the flat zones are sloped areas for movement. One zone is between the bus terminal square and the civic square in the bus terminal lobby. The second transition between the civic square and Weygand Street is programmed with an open area for temporary souks. The empty space has infrastructural points that provide services for small shops. This retail space is again a space for movement to occur.

HAMAD AL-EISA

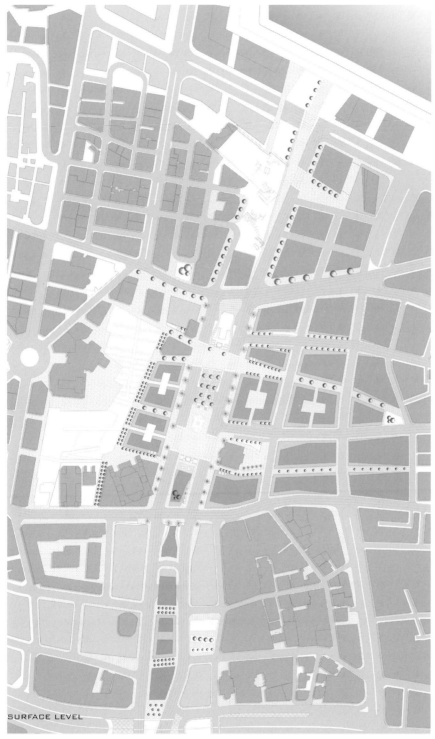

SURFACE LEVEL

02

03

01 Martyrs Square: Perspective from North showing underground parking system
02 Surface Level Plan
03 First Floor Plan

04

05

04 Plan showing parking structures in downtown and the districts they serve
05 Diagram showing underground parking structure and pedestrian networks
across the square

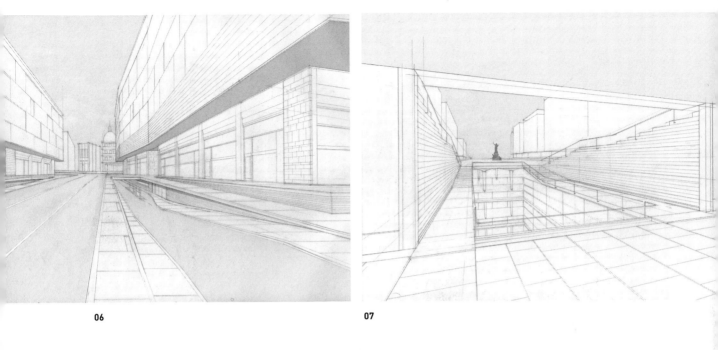

06

07

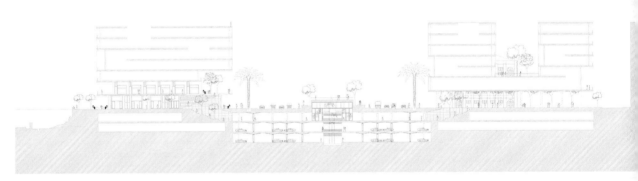

08

The parking complex is an essential part of the proposal, creating a destination as well as an entry point into the city. Vehicle entries into the complex are programmed to enhance the destination. Elements of public life that have seemingly disappeared in the area known as Solidere—gas stations, auto repair shops, car washes—are reintroduced into the underground world. Other elements of public life such as convenience stores, laundromats, tailors, and sandwich shops are once again part of the city in a concentrated area of activity. This second layer of retail and services belongs only partially to the underground world of parking. The porous articulation of the ground surface serves to fragment the line between what is below ground and what is above.

The public space proposed is transient. The urbanism does not attempt to create public life but rather sets a stage on which it can emerge.

06 Perspective showing ground level at the square and pedestrian entry point into the underground parking
07 Perspective showing lower level at the pedestrian entry point looking onto the ground level with Martyrs stations on the background
08 Martyrs Square: Transverse Section

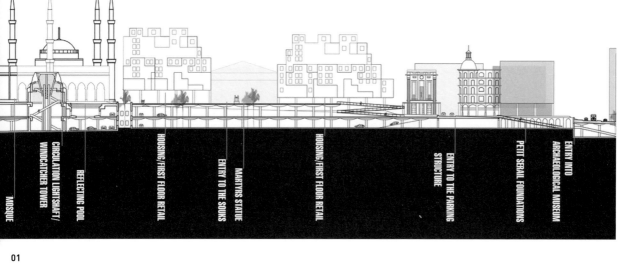

MOSQUE

CIRCULATION LIGHTSHAFT/ WINDCATCHER TOWER

REFLECTING POOL

HOUSING/FIRST FLOOR RETAIL

MARTYRS STATUE ENTRY TO THE SOUKS

HOUSING/FIRST FLOOR RETAIL

ENTRY TO THE PARKING STRUCTURE

PETIT SERAIL FOUNDATIONS

ENTRY INTO ARCHAEOLOGICAL MUSEUM

01

02

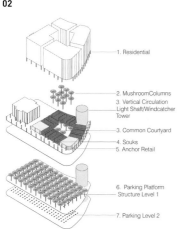

1. Residential
2. MushroomColumns
3. Vertical Circulation Light Shaft/Windcatcher Tower
3. Common Courtyard
4. Souks
5. Anchor Retail
6. Parking Platform Structure Level 1
7. Parking Level 2

The Wall proposal for Martyrs Square reveals the palimpsest of the site's history—scratching at the ruins of its surface and tracing the diverse and complex layers of its history and memory. The platform superinfrastructure accommodates a number of functions: a transportation hub; a living memorial to the city; a series of descending belvederes and pedestrian paths connecting the Beirut city center to the waterfront; an archeological museum; and finally a green corridor and surface that restitches East to West Beirut.

The parking and bus station act as a central meeting point for the BCD, a direct reference to Martyrs Square's historic function as a transportation center (the city tramline infrastructure was laid down in 1908). Beirut's modern highway system was designed around the Square as a transportation hub: the Damascus Road begins at Martyrs Square, which serves as an embarking area for buses servicing the country's mountain villages and the start of Lebanon's major highway that travels to Tripoli and Sidon. The superinfrastructure provides parking for those visiting the BCD and for inhabitants living in its adjacencies, in addition to housing an underground bus hub for the light-rail bus transit line proposed for Beirut.

The underground platform structure works with the natural topography of the site, which dramatically drops 30 meters across 900 meters from south to north. Underground platforms reveal themselves intermittently along the Martyrs Square corridor. A precedent for this layered platform is the 1934 Delahalle Plan, which proposed a link between Martyrs Square and the sea. Intermittent light wells and sunken courts vertically slice along the platform's infrastructure in section, allowing both light and vegetation below grade. This also allows for the scraping away and exposing of archeological ruins and remains. Catwalks span these exposed excavations, linking parking areas to vertical circulation paths. Intermittent "wind catchers" in the infrastructure act both as circulation and lookout towers. These wind catchers host local cultural and art installations.

The Green Line between East and West Beirut during the civil war made Martyrs Square a no-man's land. Now the stepped platform structure creates a series of cascading

SHANNON BASSETT

belvederes across the site down to the sea, creating a pedestrian path linking the Martyrs Square corridor to its east-west adjacencies down to the waterfront and proposed heritage paths.

Adjacent typologies include courtyard housing combined with first-floor retail, employing a reconstruction of souk typology. The public street colonnade and the wall are a public-private partnership.

As one contemporary historian noted, the war that is most remembered is not that of Arab insurgency against the French Mandate during the 1920s, which produced the martyrs commemorated in the Square, but the more recent civil war and the Lebanese-Israeli conflict that devastated the city of Beirut—yet these wars are still not widely discussed. This historian prescribed a mass psychotherapy session for the people of Beirut. It is hoped that The Wall will not only serve as a space for public memory but also as a vibrant urban space that resuscitates the life and hope of the city.

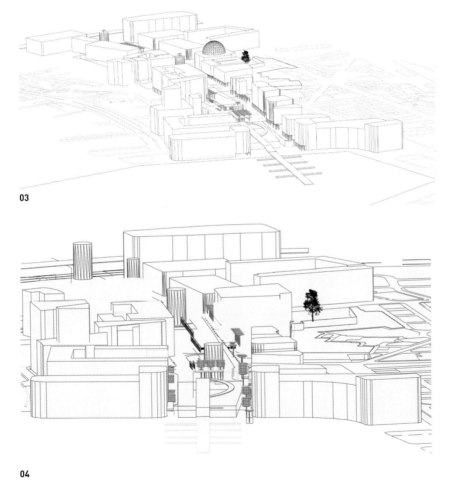

03

04

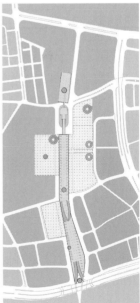

05

01 Martyrs Square: Longitudinal Section
02 Exploded axonometric of typical courtyard block
03 Perspectives from South showing large wind catchers
04 Sectional-Perspective from north
05 Parking level plan

This project draws its inspiration from Lebanese souvenirs bought in the souks of Saida, a city south of Beirut: cheap plastic lamps that are shiny, colorful, and embossed with intricate patterns. When switched on, they light up and play traditional Middle Eastern songs just a bit too loudly, which never fails to bring a smile. These objects are a great inspiration because they encapsulate the joy and irony of the culture; these qualities contribute to the vibrancy of the city, and this project seeks to infuse them into the design.

Beirut exists as a fragmented and layered city in which Martyrs Square and its recent history of war weigh heavily on the psyche of inhabitants. For that reason, this particular void in the city must be recognized as a site of memorialization. Considering how controversial the ground itself is, the decision was made to lift the memorial to a higher plane. For this, a level of abstraction is given to the memory of the site, perceivable only at a distance and not interfering with everyday activities on the ground. The memorial will marry the metropolitan scale to the immediate context with a series of towers placed along the Green Line.

These memorial towers position Martyrs Square within the larger context of Beirut and its surrounding topography, but free the ground plane of the responsibility of "memorializing." The towers will light up at night, gaining a presence in the skyline that speaks to Beirut, Lebanon, and the world beyond. The middle portion of each tower is used for solar harvesting, which provides energy for the structure. These solar devices will act as a catalyst for the city to tackle its very serious energy shortage by encouraging the use of alternative sources.

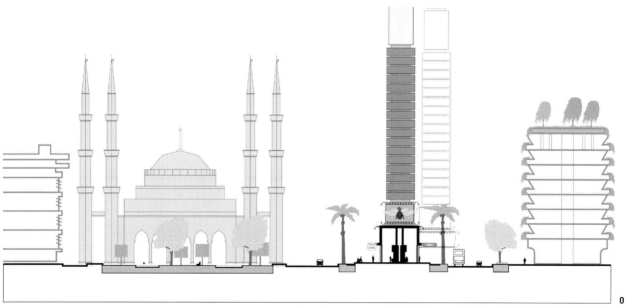

01

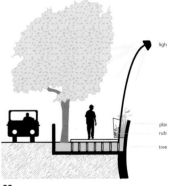

03

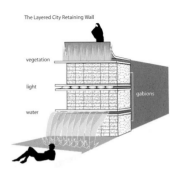

02   04

01 Martyrs Square: Transverse Section
02 Martyrs Square: Surface level plan showing connections to the waterfront
03 Sectional detail of typical sidewalk
04 Perspective detail of the layered city retaining wall

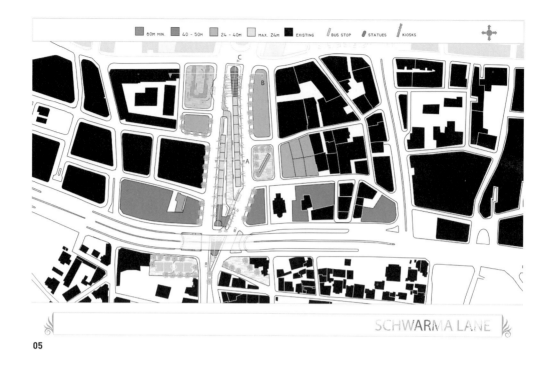

SCHWARMA LANE

05

MARTYRS' SQUARE

06

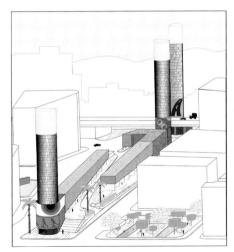

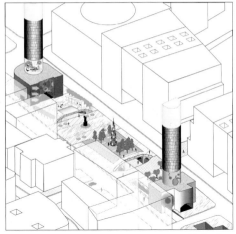

07   **08**

On the ground, the towers take on localized functions, including a taxi station, tourist information area, underground parking entrances, banking machines, and a small recycling station. They are to be covered in signage, angled specifically to capture the attention of both pedestrians and drivers moving through the site. This new signage will introduce a level of energy that invigorates the emerging public life of Beirut by popularizing the site.

The towers also act like brackets containing four distinct "episodes," which break up the site and reinforce the east-west axis. These episodes are Schwarma Lane, Martyrs Square, Archeological Terraces, and Tidal Platform. Each episode responds to the needs of present and future adjacent programs while creating unique urbanisms along the Martyrs Square axis. Three large-scale moves support these episodes.

George Haddad Street will be reconstructed into a surface street that will slow traffic and allow the adjacent neighborhood, Gemmayze, to begin infiltrating the site from the east.

Solidere's proposed tall buildings at the waterfront are to be repositioned and redistributed inland, placing medium-height mixed-use buildings along the water to create a buffer from the congested Trieste Street leading north without blockading potential waterfront activities.

Each building is required to dedicate 20 percent of the exterior to green space, in a combination of plazas, terraces, roof gardens and flower boxes, to better filter the increasing amounts of dust and pollution, and to help cooling in such a hot climate.

05 Plan showing elevation planning for the Schwarma Lane
06 Plan showing elevation planning for the Martyrs Square
07 Perspective drawing showing the Schwarma Lane
08 Plan showing the Martyrs Square flanked by two towers

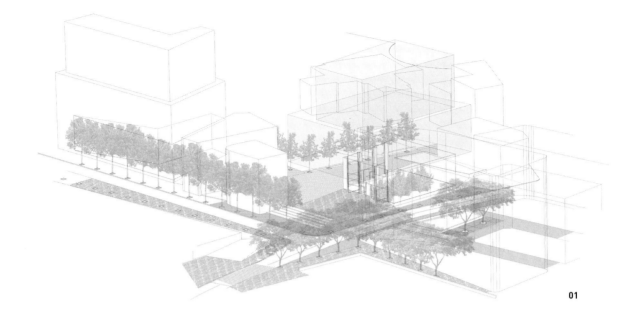

01

Envisioning a World's Capital for the Twenty-first Century immediately brings up the notion of large scale. The city should be thought of as a megablock structure. Pieces typologically, morphologically, and programmatically distinct from one another are clustered together. The remaining spaces, the "gaps," are where public activity—urbanity—emerges.

Martyrs Square should become not only the square for the city of Beirut but the focal point for Lebanese society as a whole. Located at the edge of the Green Line, it represents the point where two cultures join as a unified entity. This heavily charged symbolic space has an immediate impact on the configuration of the built environment. The urban structure needs to be scaled appropriately to the level of symbolism present in the collective memory of the site.

Any particular space is limited not by its actual edges but by the perception of apparent boundaries. A space of this nature cannot be reduced to its physical limits. Elements from the immediate urban surroundings should be pulled into the space. The towers of the new financial and hotel district, the Grand Serail, and distant views of the ocean and mountains are just a few of the elements that are important to the perception of the Square.

Urban activity flourishes in the gaps left by the superblock structure. These sequences of irregular spaces that redefine the edges of the blocks stitch together in a meandering surface. This surface penetrates the base of the building, blurring the defined and rigid structure of the Square as it is today. To the south, the system expands to integrate the Square with the fabric at the other side of the highway, in particular with the Monot district, already a vibrant center for metropolitan life. The highway is seen as an asset more than a boundary that separates the central district from the rest of the city. It represents a vantage

AARON COHEN

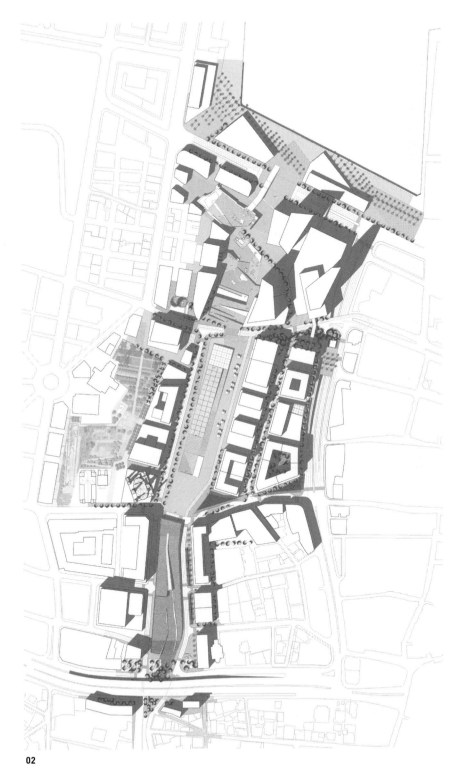

02

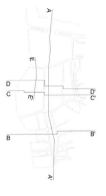

03

01 Axonometric view of a "gap" space
02 Martyrs Square: Site plan

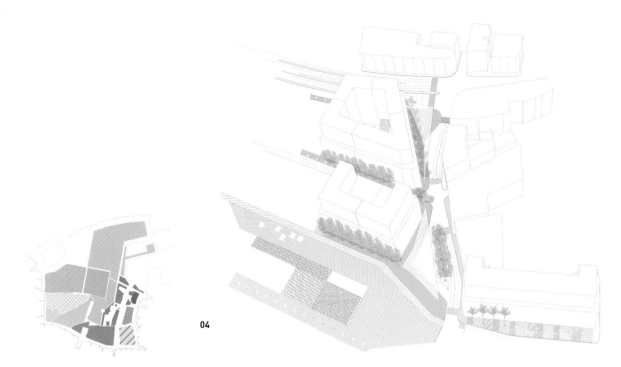

04

05

point from which the vastness of the Square, the axis, and the city is perceived in its magnitude—a quality that the project emphasizes. By placing a landscaped building, the Contemporary Art and Media Center/Beirut INFO-BOX, in the south segment of the axis, a similar viewpoint is provided to pedestrians without breaking the continuity of the surface.

The archeological remains become an active part of the system rather than objects of contemplation. Pedestrians will be active players instead of simple spectators. The remains generate an elaborate landscape of limits, edges, boundaries, and perspectives that enrich the intended meandering experience.

The ceremonial aspect of the Square is treated differently and is full of symbolic elements. It appears delimited by a covered patio, recreating the exact perimeter of the Square prior to the demolition of the Petit Serail. The platform generates a key vantage point; the ground level around it disappears and the elements mentioned before seem closer. The statue is placed before the third patio, reflecting its important role as a symbolic element.

04 Perspective view of a "gap" space and its relationship to Martyrs Square
05 Axonometric view of a "gap" space
06 Martyrs Square: Transverse Section BB[1]
07 Martyrs Square: Transverse Section CC[1]
08 Martyrs Square: Transverse Section DD[1]

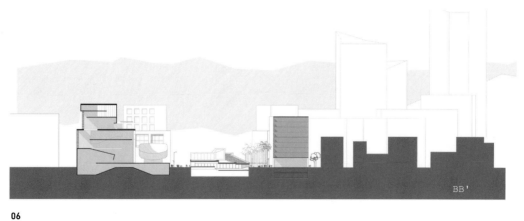

06

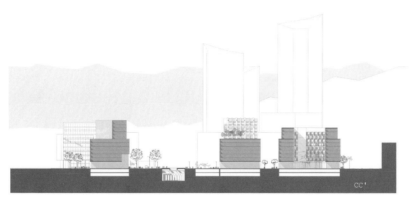

07

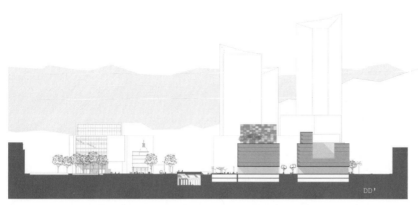

08

This project allows Martyrs Square to act as meeting point in the city, with the introduction of a transit hub along its southern edge. The Corniche and its unique urban life are pulled into Martyrs Square from the north. The activities in the north and south culminate in a variety of cultural institutions at the Square. Initially, four urban elements were mapped: transportation routes, boundaries, institutions, and open spaces. These were presented at three different scales: Beirut City, Beirut Central District (BCD), and Martyrs Square. These initial mappings are critical to the conceptualization of this urban vision. By taking into account existing transportation, boundary, institutional, and open-space conditions, the project materialized into a master plan. With the introduction of a much-needed meeting place and cultural destination, these elements ultimately inspired the ensuing moments of intersection that express Beirut's dynamic urban realm.

The transportation mapping pinpoints the major thoroughfares that range from primary to secondary and tertiary. This transportation hub will house local bus lines, taxi stands, associated waiting and ticketing areas, potential light-rail stops, shopping, and entertainment. The primary conceptual framework for the project is the macro-weaving and micro-weaving of diverse yet closely related program uses. In the macro-weaving diagram, the three primary weaves occur at the three traffic intersections along Martyrs Square's axis. The first is an overlap of transportation and botanic garden, the second of botanic garden and institutions, and the third of institutions (archeology museum), open space (archeology park), and waterfront. The plan shows how this urban intervention integrates with the surrounding fabric. The transportation hub at the southern portion of the plan is linked to associated program uses with pedestrian bridges that frame the southern entry sequence into the Square. To the east of the transit hub, Debbas Square contains underground parking and acts as an anchor to the immediate area with a monumental circulation tower.

As the transit hub's waiting areas gradually become an exterior bridge, their heavy vegetation acts as an interlude to the macro-weaving of transportation and botanical garden. In addition to being educational, the garden serves travelers as a waiting area that

02

overlooks the continuously changing yet historically significant Martyrs Square. The Square is flanked on the west by a museum associated with the Garden of Forgiveness and on the east by a school, library, and retail (ground floor) and residential (upper floors) uses. The plan clearly indicates a strong east-west connection by maintaining an axial clearing that stretches from the Etoile monument to the Sacre Coeur School in Gemmayze.

The second macro-weave occurs at the Petit Serail, where the remaining foundations are preserved to become a sunken entry-court to the underground archeology museum, which leads to the archeology park. The final macro-weave occurs where the archeology park bridges under Port Street to the waterfront, with its associated office, retail, and recreational activities.

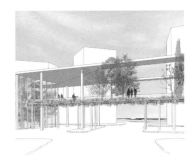

03

04

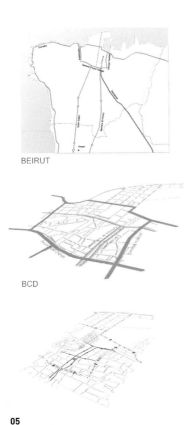

BEIRUT

BCD

05

06

---

01 Perspective drawing showing the waiting area for the transportation hub
02 Martyrs Square: Model of Archeology Park
03 View of overpass linking transportation hub to Martyrs Square
04 "Macro-weaving" diagram showing three primary traffic intersections along Martyrs Square axis

05 Transportation diagrams showing major thoroughfares (primary, secondary and tertiary) presented at three different scales: Beirut City, Beirut Central District (BCD), and Martyrs Square
06 Martyrs Square: Site plan

01

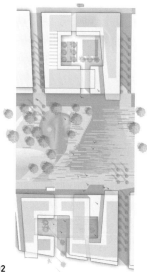

02

This project aims to introduce a new building typology and program to Martyrs Square while extending the green axis well beyond the site to the south toward Damascus. The main square is imagined as the site of a new urban campus, where student itineraries intermingle with those of the general population, adding diversity and increased activity to the city center. The addition of a tram system, which has historical precedents in the Square, will link Martyrs Square to disparate parts of the city along the Corniche edge and in a loop of the downtown, in the hopes of encouraging Beirutis to visit this historic space in the city. The tram proposal addresses traffic congestion, reducing automobile traffic through the Square. The eventual completion of the tram system will combine with other modes of transportation (buses, taxis), which extend beyond the metropolitan region to other parts of Lebanon in the north and south.

The campus program directly adjacent to the Square will occupy a six-story courtyard building typology with open accessible centers that serve multiple purposes. First, the open centers allow for an extension of the public activities occurring in the Square to filter into and engage the programs of the campus. Second, while upper-level programs are reserved for institutional use, the ground floors will remain public, with mainly restaurant and retail occupancies. Finally, this new typology will work interactively with Martyrs Square and its natural topography as a system of rainwater collection and distribution for the district. The courtyard buildings along the Square will be required to maintain 25 percent of programmable space on each roof, while the remaining 75 percent will serve as

DAVID FLETCHER

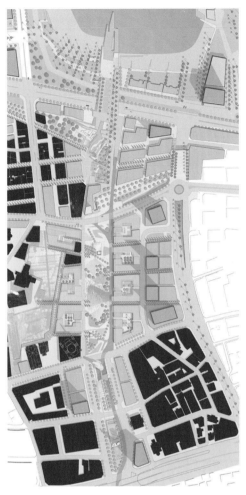

03

04

05

green roof space for the collection of rainwater. The runoff is collected and stored in cisterns below each courtyard for distributing back into the buildings and for maintaining and enriching water features along the main square.

The design of the Square mixes natural landscape topographies with paved plazas and pedestrian routes, which give coherence along the north-south axis as well as connect campus programs across the Square. This strategy welcomes the addition of the tramline through the space and provides a flexible system to locate stops. As the Square descends into the archeology near the water, several new east-west axes are introduced as a way to negotiate the topography and structure the site for new buildings. The project utilizes the natural change in topography to connect a land bridge from the archeology to the waterfront, relieving the grade crossing by pedestrians. The waterfront is edged with recreational, retail, and open-space programs, and the shoreline is extended into the harbor in the form of an urban beach.

01 Perspective showing paved plaza in Martyrs Square
02 Plan of two blocks across Martyrs Square with proposed courtyard building typologies
03 Martyrs Square: Site plan
04 Site plan of proposed east west axes
05 3D drawing showing the urban beach in the background

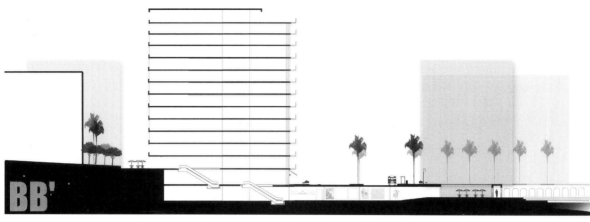

01

02

The role of Beirut's Corniche as a physical barrier against the Mediterranean is secondary to its role in promoting social interaction. For years the lengthy and winding sea wall has functioned as a primary source of the city's social cohesion. Despite its position on Beirut's periphery, the Corniche has played and should continue to play a central part in the city's life.

A sense of neutrality is paramount to successfully rebuilding Beirut. Beirut's culturally rich and diverse population needs a place where it can be joined and interact; the waterfront offers the perfect staging area for this purpose. Unfortunately, developers have largely failed to exploit the promise of the Corniche. In its current role, the Corniche inhibits rather than facilitates public-ness and interaction in the city it surrounds. The presence of the Lebanese military, which recently occupied the vast public waterfront directly north of Martyrs Square, reduces the appeal of the waterfront. At the critical axis set up by the Green Line, a potentially fruitful and exciting draw of pedestrians to the waterfront dead-ends at the vehicular Corniche road and a barricaded military zone. For years the Green Line has separated the Christian and Muslim neighborhoods of Beirut. The line bisects Martyrs Square and continues down to the water. The Square's metaphorical neutrality should be extended further to the waterfront, where the line is dissolved.

Although Beirut's urban fabric remains a patchwork, a movement toward developing axiality in the city is clearly present. This alignment should be spatially elaborated to give the public a sense of procession that leads it to the waterfront. With a few stops along the way, the procession should climax by the water and aid in the definition of a new public space. Activity should be relocated to the waterfront, making the old public space at Martyrs Square commemorative.

To create a sense of arrival at the waterfront while simultaneously creating a point of departure, a flow among open spaces throughout the city, the pedestrian network, and the Corniche needs to be created. Developing a strategic pedestrian network that weaves through the city and connects open spaces without obstructing the flow is essential. A transportation hub, encouraging mass transit and discouraging car traffic, should be created near the waterfront to bring commuters to Beirut via land as well as water. Adding activities along the waterfront will be necessary to keep the public interested in this burgeoning area. Using the city's natural seaward slope will assist in creating this procession to the water with a few stops along the axial way. It is also critical to establish a balance between vehicular and pedestrian traffic. This can be achieved by creating more paths—both those that isolate pedestrians and those that are more integrated into vehicular traffic. Sunken courts and underpasses, and a system of pedestrian escalators, would all contribute to bringing pedestrians to the water. The Corniche, as proposed by Solidere, should pass through the city to create a shortcut for both cars and pedestrians.

Finally, relocating the new public square to the waterfront—the new nexus of activity and diversity—creates a unique type of public space that all the people of Beirut can embrace and make their own. The neutrality of this zone will inevitably spread into the city by means of both the axes and by filtering into adjacent areas of Beirut, including the old public square. In this proposal, Martyrs Square becomes commemorative in a way that allows for reflection on days gone by without holding Beirut in its past. A large reflective pool will mark where the public square once stood and where civil war once took its toll.

05

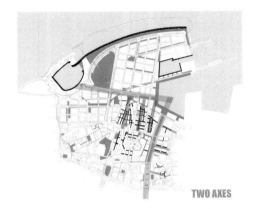

TWO AXES

03

04

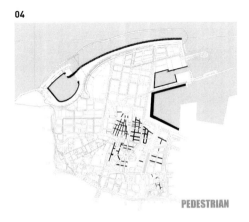

PEDESTRIAN

01 Martyrs Square: Longitudinal section leading to watercourt
02 Site diagrams showing existing condition and proposed waterfront public square
03 Diagram showing the intersection of the main two main two axes at the waterfront
04 Diagram showing pedestrian networks
05 Martyrs Square: Site plan

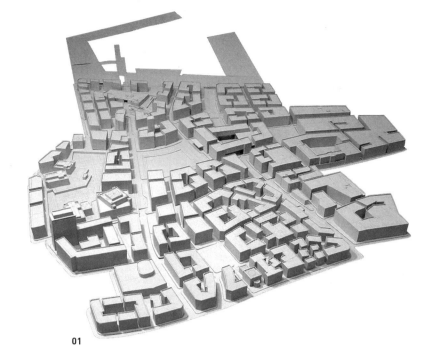

01

02

03

Social, religious, and political divisions have played a major role in both the symbolic and physical presence of Martyrs Square for the people of Beirut. The history of Martyrs Square includes its service as a battlefield and political dividing line between East and West Beirut during the civil war. The result was the physical destruction of the Square and almost all of the surrounding buildings and infrastructure. The Square remains undefined spatially and programmatically. Proposals for the redevelopment of the Square suggest a long axial space flanked by major city roads that run north and south. This would merely mimic its previous configuration and reinforce the spatial and cognitive separation of the city into two halves. The intense traffic along the Square would discourage pedestrian use and add to the noise and pollution of the space.

Confronting the Square's history as a political and physical division in the city led to challenging the axial nature of the proposed new square and attempting to reorient the space to create a more usable public center that reconnects East and West Beirut. Can cities be physically shaped to mediate social and political divisions? The project intends to create a new public space that strengthens connections between different neighborhoods of the city and reestablishes the primacy of Martyrs Square as the city's main urban space.

The goal of the project is to create an urban space of public convergence, accessible to all social groups, that encourages both spontaneous and planned public activities. The urban strategy is to create a very large open space, highly accessible but legible as a cohesive space. The new space, roughly equal in length on all sides, is spatially connected to the surrounding areas though improved street configurations and view corridors. With no predominant orientation, the Square acts as a physical center rather than dividing the city. The large size of the Square will allow for multiplicity and diversity of people and activities and lessen the ability of any one social group to appropriate the entire space. The size will

SAMUEL OLBEKSON

allow for a mixing of different scales of activity throughout the day and night, fostering a new identity for Beirut.

Predominantly hard-surfaced, the space would be highly flexible and open to many activities, including markets, concerts, and festivals. Green space and seating areas within the Square would encourage daily use and provide shade. Places for vendors and performers would draw people of all social groups to the Square. The surrounding city fabric will be densified, spatially enclosing the site but allowing for greater physical access to the Square. A mix of programmatic elements will be encouraged that engage the various public constituencies of Beirut. Museums, galleries, and other public institutions will coexist with office and residential spaces. Government and religious facilities will exist outside of the Square.

Beirut's inherent diversity and history of social conflict provided inspiration for this project. The space will be viewed as a shared public amenity, not an isolated pocket of any singular activity or population group. Recreated as a vital urban center, Martyrs Square will provide a signature urban space for Beirut and the eastern Mediterranean region.

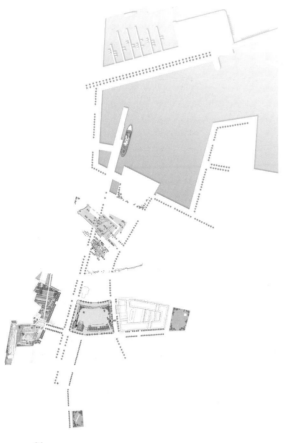

04

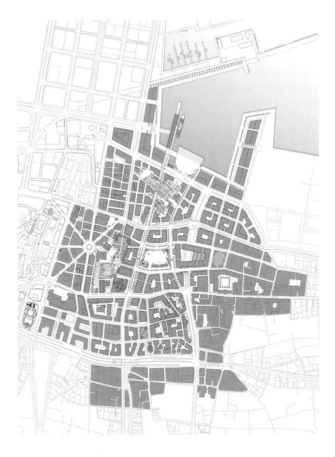

05

01 View of model from waterfront
02 View of model from the south
03 Map showing east-west divide of Beirut along Martyrs Square axis
04 Martyrs Square: Diagram showing open public spaces
05 Martyrs Square: Site plan

In an urban society such as Beirut's, with increasingly diverse citizens whose social conditions are constantly changing, it is impossible for the authorities to predetermine how public spaces should perform. Instead, the design of public space needs to facilitate the expression of varied collective and individual voices. This direction in public space design enables the underrepresented to become visible in society and increases their ability to participate in public debate.

The project searches for a new form of public open space that could maximize participation in private activities. Conventionally an open space acts as a pocket, a vacant lot surrounded by vertical buildings. The buildings that directly influence the formation of open space are those immediately adjacent to it, and the numbers of buildings and the kinds of programs allowed to participate are usually limited. If this vertical pocket of open space were rotated 90 degrees and allowed to expand, a new horizontal public space would be created and the participating buildings would multiply greatly without sacrificing valuable real estate. Using Brasilia's city planning as a precedent, this type of intervention could be achieved by simple rules and regulations for securing public space. However, 90-degree rotation of public space, made possible by lifting buildings on pilotis, does not necessarily allow the private activities to shape public life. That is why the private programs need to be pulled down from buildings or pushed up from the ground to activate the newly formed spaces. These activities would fill Martyrs Square, inviting passersby to participate. These elements would be visible from the other buildings and would begin to connect and coordinate life in the Square.

This proposed public space affects the city in new ways. It marks a horizontal datum that generates a sense of continuity throughout the Martyrs Square area, allowing

YUTAKA SHO

increased formal freedom to individual building design. Also, the new horizontal space frames the views of the city differently. The conventional city grid frames the view by placing an object at the end of an axis, giving the object a symbolic significance from a single point of view. The panoramic horizontal view, on the other hand, allows multiple objects to be seen simultaneously by multiple viewers, creating associations between disparate monuments. For example, the martyrs statue could be seen sometimes with the memorial statue of Christian and Muslim conflict, sometimes with the mosque, sometimes with the churches; each time the statue leads the viewer to reflect on the past a bit differently.

The final design resolution succeeds in expanding Martyrs Square beyond its physical limits while preserving the Square's recognizable form. In doing so, it is able to include all citizens of Beirut in a collective effort to recreate the city's public life, lost during the war, and encourage a multivocal yet unified society.

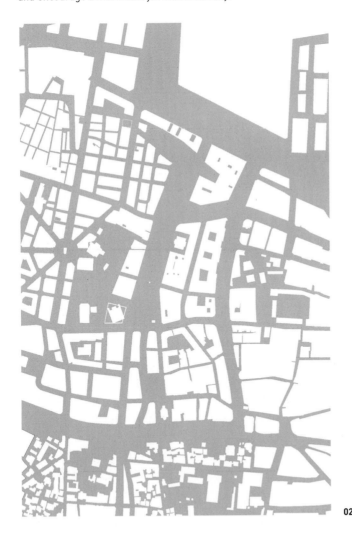

02

03

01 Perspective showing 90-degree rotated public space and lifted museum building
02 Figure ground showing cores in relation to footprints
03 Martyrs Square piloti level plan

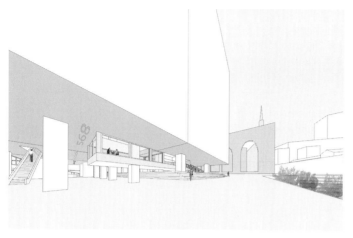

04

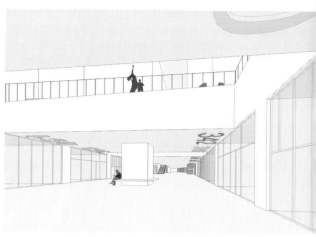

05

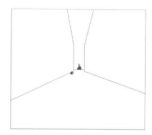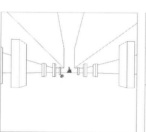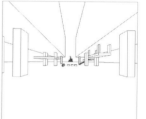

06

07-08

04 Perspective of public building lobby along the square
05 Perspective showing passage under Martyrs Square
06 Perspective diagram showing transformation of attitude
towards street and public space
07-08 Martyrs Square: Longitudinal section

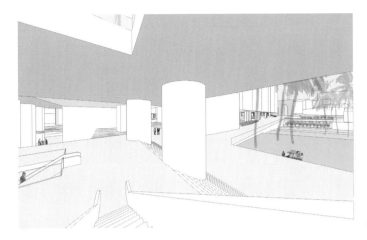

09

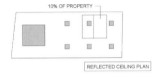

10% OF PROPERTY

REFLECTED CEILING PLAN

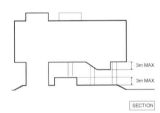

3m MAX

3m MAX

SECTION

ALIGN W/ ADJACENT BUILDING

STREET ELEVATION

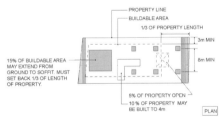

PROPERTY LINE
BUILDABLE AREA
1/3 OF PROPERTY LENGTH
3m MIN
8m MIN

15% OF BUILDABLE AREA
MAY EXTEND FROM
GROUND TO SOFFIT. MUST
SET BACK 1/3 OF LENGTH
OF PROPERTY.

5% OF PROPERTY OPEN
10 % OF PROPERTY MAY
BE BUILT TO 4m

PLAN

TYPE 1:
INSTITUTIONAL / LARGE CORPORATE
ADJACENT TO MARTYRS SQUARE.
MATCH PAVING WITH CITY STANDARD.

10

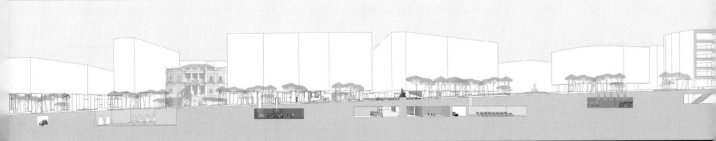

09 Perspective showing public spaces in relation to buildings lifted on pilotis
10 Diagrams describing guidelines for buildings lifted on pilotis

Part 2: Istanbul   Intermodal Istanbul, Sirkeci Square

TANSEL KORKMAZ

ON THE REGENERATION
OF THE GOLDEN HORN

ARCHITECTURAL INTERVENTION WITHIN A HISTORICAL CONTEXT

Intervention within a historical context is always a challenge for architects. The main concern is almost never the context itself, but the presence of the past—the presence of an absence. A context that has historical significance is haunted; it captivates the architect with its lost "original" image. This sense of loss or absence prompts the desire for wholeness, a restoration of the loss. The craving for an impossible wholeness is behind the common tendency to conceive of the context of the intervention as either a fetish or a harbor of fantasies.

THE MULTILAYERED NATURE OF THE GOLDEN HORN

> Though all other cities have their periods of government and are subject to the decays of time, Constantinople alone seems to claim a kind of immortality and will continue to be a city as long as humanity shall live either to inhabit or rebuild it.
>
> **Pierre Gilles**, *French Humanist* (1550)[1]

Istanbul has many historical layers: the Late Roman/Pagan, Byzantine/Christian, Ottoman/Muslim, and modern Turkish. All have inscribed their traces on the city. The dominance of different cultures is reflected in its successive names: Byzantion, Constantinopolis, Istanbul. Except for the newly developed suburban areas (such as Çekmece, Beylikdüzü, Kozyatağı, Ümraniye, Kemerburgaz, Çekmeköy), Istanbul presents one of the world's most intricate urban cultures to its inhabitants and visitors. The first settlements of the city date back to the late third millennium B.C. It was the capital of the Byzantine empire for 1,000 years (330–1453) and then of the Ottoman empire for almost 500 years. It owes its continued existence and cosmopolitan culture to its advantageous geographical position: a fertile hinterland and convenient harbor at the intersection of major historical routes—at the crossroads of the Black Sea and the Mediterranean, of Europe and Asia. In its long history, it has experienced periods of stagnation and crisis as well as of rise and glory, but has always survived—despite great earthquakes, fires, epidemics, and invasions—without any rupture, even during the Middle Ages. There were some periods within this historical continuity when it became one of the largest cities of Europe and the Middle East[2]: in the fifth and sixth centuries, in the eleventh and twelfth centuries, and in the seventeenth century. Its unique topography explains its legendary attraction.

01 Aerial photograph showing areas of intervention along the Golden Horn

To the right, Galata, her foreground a forest of masts and flags; above Galata and Pera, the imposing shapes of her European palaces outlined against the sky; in front, the bridge connecting the two banks, across which flow continually two opposite, many-hued streams of life; to the left; Stambul, scattered over her seven hills, each crowned with a gigantic mosque with its leaden dome and gilded pinnacle. . . the sky, in which are blended together the most delicate shades of blue and silver, throws everything into marvelous relief, while the water, of a sapphire blue and dotted over with little purple buoys, reflects the minarets in long trembling lines of white; the cupolas glisten in the sunlight; all that mass of vegetation sways and palpitates in the morning air. . . To deny this is the

most beautiful sight on earth would be churlish indeed, as ungrateful toward God as it would be unjust to his creation; and it is certain that anything more beautiful would surpass mankind's powers of enjoyment.
Edmondo De Amicis, *Constantinople* (1896)[3]

From the seventh to the nineteenth century, the settlements lay on three pieces of land separated from each other by the sea: the historical peninsula, the Galata (the south and north side of the Golden Horn's mouth), and Üsküdar, on the Asiatic side of the Bosphorus. The historical peninsula was the center of the city and kept its importance up to the nineteenth century and then lost its primacy to Galata and Rue de Pera (Istiklal Caddesi) and to the Bosphorus. Thus the Golden Horn has held the generative nucleus of the city from the beginning. The present context is an intricate web fabricated over the course of 3,000 years by different cultures. To gain an understanding of the true nature of the Golden Horn, there are basically five historical layers to be analyzed in their complex relationship: Byzantion, Constantinopolis, and Istanbul (pre-modern, modern, and post-1980s).

BYZANTION
Byzas, the founder of the city, gave his name to it: Byzantion.[4] The harbor Neorion (Eminönü-Sirkeci) and the Acropolis (on the first hill and at the same time at the highest point of the historical peninsula, where Topkapı Palace is located today) are the legacy of Byzantion and have endured as focal

02 Istanbul Modern: Building 4 of the Galata port was converted into a museum of modern art (photo: Cemal Emden)

03 The Rahmi Koç Museum houses the private collection of industrial products and machinery of the Koç family, prominent Turkish industrialists (photo: Cemal Emden)

points of the city over thousands of years. This continuity owes much to the merit of Greek urbanization ideals: bringing forth the potential of the site and establishing harmony with the topography. The city became a project of the Roman Emperor Septimus Severus as a local symbol of his universal power. He initiated the lasting urban structure of the city with two artifacts: the Forum Tetrastoon and the first part of the *mese,* the middle street, the *embolos* connecting the forum to the city gate.[5] The *mese* is today's Divanyolu and is still one of the most important arteries of the peninsula. He also began to build the Hippodrome, but could not complete it because of its ambitious layout that challenged the topography; Constantine completed it.

CONSTANTINOPOLIS

Constantine transferred the capital of the Roman empire from Rome to Byzantion, the "New Rome," in 330. What the Eastern Roman empire did in terms of urbanization was not a radical transformation but a development and enrichment of the existing structure. Constantine kept the important urban public spaces of the city: the harbor/Neorion, at the mouth of the Golden Horn; the *mese,* the main artery of the city connecting the city center to the city gate; the Forum Tetrastoon; and the Hippodrome.[6] Furthermore, he enlarged the city as the new capital of the Christian empire; built new city

04a View of Silahtarağa at the tip of the Golden Horn (photo: Cemal Emden)

04b Santral Istanbul: The Silahtarağa power plant is to be converted for use by Istanbul Bilgi University (photo: Cemal Emden)

05 Sütlüce Slaughterhouse: A project is under way to turn the old slaughterhouse into an international congress and cultural center (photo: Cemal Emden)

06 Feshane, an old textile factory, converted to an international congress and cultural center (photo: Cemal Emden)

walls, the Wall of Constantine; and designed a network of fan-shaped main arteries and some secondary streets perpendicular to them.[7] The *mese* extended toward the west, bifurcated at almost the middle of the peninsula and then its two arms reached the city gates in the new walls. The southern arm was used as the triumphal way and articulated accordingly; it was embellished with a chain of open public spaces. Augusteion and the Forum of Constantine were built by Constantine; in the fourth and the fifth centuries followed the Forum Tauri, the Forum Bovis, and the Forum Arcadii. Constantine's major monument, the Church of Hagia Sophia (rebuilt by Justinian), kept its importance as a spiritual focal point in Ottoman Istanbul as well as in modern times. It was Theodosius II, in the fifth century, who once more enlarged the city toward the west and built new city walls: the Wall of Theodosius.

07 Fener-Balat, a rejuvenated district under the joint program of the European Union and Fatih municipality, expected to be completed by 2006

Beginning with the tenth century, the presence of foreign communities became an issue for the city. Italian merchants' activities increased: the Amalfians, the Venetians, the Pisans, and the Genoese acquired territorial concessions and settled around the harbor, the Neorion/Eminönü-Sirkeci. This was the beginning of the multicultural urban life that has been one of the assets of the city ever since. Müller-Wiener points out that in the twelfth

08 Cibali Tobacco Factory, designed by Vallaury in the 1880s, now houses the Kadir Has University, completed in 2001 (photo: Cemal Emden)

century, visitors estimated the population of foreigners to be 12,000. Jews were segregated and settled in the west of Galata. In the thirteenth century, the Genoese built their own settlements in old Sykai (Galata), Pera, following the grid plan.[8] It was crucial as a beginning of the difference between the urban structure of the historical peninsula and of Galata, a difference that became more visible in Ottoman Istanbul. No other major structural changes were made by any emperor, except for adding some new monuments and polishing and articulating the existing urban structure.

Thus Constantine managed to develop and embellish Byzantion's structure and turn it into an imperial city, Constantinopolis: a spiritual, cultural, commercial, and administrative center of the empire. The urban structure he developed carried on until the city became the capital of the Ottoman Empire, and most of its traces persisted even after that: the first part of the *mese* is today's Divanyolu, still one of the important axes of the peninsula; the Hippodrome is today's Atmeydanı, and Forum Tauri is today's Beyazıt Meydanı, both still important open spaces of the peninsula; there is the Fatih Külliyesi where the Havariyyun church once stood; and the harbor was used until the 1950s. Today, however, few buildings remain from the Byzantine period, making it difficult to envisage what the city looked like. It is nonetheless one of the major constituent layers of the collective memory of the city and holds the invisible structure of the peninsula.

09 Miniatürk, opened in 2003, is a park along the Golden Horn that presents miniature versions of historic sites of Istanbul, Anatolia, and former Ottoman provinces; it was inspired by Moduradam in the Netherlands, one of the earliest miniature parks, which was opened in 1952 (photo: Cemal Emden)

ISTANBUL

In 1453, Fatih (Mehmet II) conquered Istanbul and declared it the new capital of his empire. It was an Islamic empire, that is, an entirely different dwelling culture; consequently some structural changes within the city had to take place. Two urgent issues were on the sultan's agenda: reconstruction of the city walls and repopulation. Using repopulation strategies, he managed to increase the population to 65,000–80,000 around 1480: Turks constituted 58 percent, Greeks 23 percent, Franks, Armenians, and Jews 19 percent.[9] These ratios and their almost stable profile up to the late nineteenth century, sustaining the multicultural nature of the city, should be seen as a natural outcome of empire.[10]

As an Islamic city, Istanbul had a different urban structure than Constantinople. Instead of a structure based on an urban skeleton containing open spaces and primary monuments (i.e., colossal arteries connecting huge public spaces and monuments), it became a multicentered structure: self-sufficient quarters organized around a *külliye*.[11] A *külliye* can be thought of as a kind of community center built by sultans or dignitaries, which contains a mosque, *medrese* (school), hospital, soup kitchen, caravanserai, *hamam* (public bath), and *bedesten* (shops); the courtyards of the complex served as the main open spaces of the city. The *külliye* was both the structural and social center of residential quarters. Against the city's impressive scale, perfect stone construction, and corresponding order, the *külliye* created a contrast with its wooden construction and the humble scale of the ordinary houses and their spontaneous, intricate context. Within this urban pattern, there was no place for colossal arteries and open spaces. Furthermore, with the augmentation in population in the sixteenth century, the peninsula became more crowded and the Byzantine arteries began to be encroached on and lost their clear-cut outline. As a result, the Byzantine urban skeleton lost its function of holding the city together, but most of its traces have survived and have triggered later interventions.

Ottoman sultans built their *külliye*s on the hills of the historical peninsula. This crowning of hills with great domes and fragile minarets emphasizes the topography—discloses the true nature of the place and its hidden inner potentials—and endows the city with a silhouette that endorses the fact that Istanbul is a Muslim city and that the Golden Horn is the setting of this city. Fatih built his *külliye* on the site of the Havariyyun church, the church of

10 a Eminönü: One of the busiest squares of Istanbul, which went through several interventions (photo: Cemal Emden)

Constantine, and began to use Edirnekapı, instead of the Golden Gate, as the city gate. This operation displaced the center of gravity in the city, and the northern branch of the *mese* became the primary axis instead of the Byzantine triumphal way leading to the Golden Gate. The northern axis would later be emphasized by other *külliye*s. Nevertheless, as the harbor[12] in Eminönü-Sirkeci stayed in its place and the area between the harbor and Divanyolu (the *mese*) was still occupied by commerce (some parts of the Grand Bazaar were already completed), the first part of the *mese* remained an important axis connecting the new central market (Grand Bazaar) to the constant spiritual center, Hagia Sophia. Beyazıt II built his *külliye* on the site of the Byzantine Forum Tauri. Either in the form of conversion, as in the case of Hagia Sophia, or of rebuilding, as in the cases of Fatih and Beyazıt *Külliye*s, these operations obviously were strategies to appropriate the territory. Constantinopolis soon became history, and with their special dwelling strategies, Ottomans managed to shape a new city: Istanbul. Although the land-use pattern of the city did not alter too much, the change in urban structure resulted in a change in the image of the city.

In Byzantion and Constantinopolis, urban life was organized within the city walls of the peninsula and of Galata; there were only country villages outside the walls. The Golden Horn was a perfect microcosm holding oppositions gracefully: the vitality of urban life within the city walls versus idyllic country life outside the walls, the calculated beauty of the architecture of public spaces versus the pastoral beauty of untouched nature. This inspiring tension continued, to a great extent, in fifteenth-century Istanbul. There were few exceptions, such as Eyüp (on the southern side of the Golden Horn), which became a significant religious center for the whole Islamic world after 1453. Besides the mausoleum for Ebu Eyüp el Ensari—the flag-bearer of the Prophet Muhammad—most mausoleums of respected religious and scientific men are in Eyüp. The existence of two important *külliye*s (Eyüp Sultan Külliyesi and Zal Mahmut Külliyesi) stressed once more the spiritual importance of the place. Eyüp thus was one of the first settlements outside the walls. In the sixteenth century, the rapid population growth was mostly absorbed within the walls and made the urban pattern denser. The shipyard that was constructed on the northern shore to the west of Galata triggered a new settlement there: Kasımpaşa. There were other military constructions in Kağıthane. Thus the silhouette and urban pattern of the northern and southern shores became significantly different: the silhouette in the former was defined mainly by shipyards, the Galata tower, and military constructions, while in the latter it was delineated by the harbor and *külliye*s.[13] On the peninsula, the character of the urban fabric was defined by the contrast between the orderly monumental *külliye*s and intricate residential pattern, between the heaviness and permanence of stone and the lightness and ephemerality of the wooden structures; in Galata there was a more homogeneous fabric made up of the grid plan and masonry buildings.

In the seventeenth and eighteenth centuries, a new dwelling pattern emerged along the shore, particularly in Kağıthane. With the influence of the French Baroque, some splendid wooden palaces and gardens were built on the waterfront. This change had already begun in the sixteenth century, but accelerated during the Tulip Era (1718–30). The Tulip Era's conceptualization and articulation of palaces and gardens pointed to an important shift in landscape culture. But a brutal mass revolt brought an end to the era and destroyed most of the palaces and gardens. Nevertheless, Kağıthane was inscribed in the collective memory of the city as the place for recreation. The period also witnessed the gradual prosperity of Galata and beyond it, Pera. As opposed to the hermetic density of the fabric within the city walls, Pera was known for vineyards up to the eighteenth century, when it became the locus of the luxurious residences of ambassadors and other wealthy non-Muslims.

In the nineteenth century, with its vivid urban life and culture, Grand Rue de Pera was a modest replica of well-known western models.

The spread of modern industry accelerated toward the mid-nineteenth century. As a natural safe harbor, the Golden Horn shore acted as a magnet for industry. The palaces and gardens built during and after the Tulip Era were gradually replaced with industrial buildings. Industry invited new settlements along the shore, and regular ferry service supported this development: Kasımpaşa, Piripaşa, Hasköy, and Sütlüce began to define a continuous fabric outside the walls.

The decline of the empire in the eighteenth and nineteenth centuries paved the way for the deterioration of the peninsula in the nineteenth century. Galata became the finance center of the city, Pera the modern cultural center, and the Bosphorus the locus of government. The dissolution of the pious foundation system (the *imaret* system), the main urbanization strategy behind the prosperity of the city, also triggered urban decay. Although the same period witnessed wide-ranging modernization efforts in the capital cities of Europe, Istanbul had neither a fresh, comprehensive vision nor enough capital to realize radical transformations; it could manage only incremental attempts at westernization.

Ironically, the great fires were almost the only urban generators of rebuilding activities. The biggest ones, the 1856 Aksaray and 1865 Hocapaşa fires, pointed up two imperatives: masonry instead of wooden construction should be adopted, and a regular street network should be established. Consequently, the historical peninsula underwent some fragmentary modernization attempts during the nineteenth century: regularization of the fabric by means of the construction of new arteries and expansion of existing ones; cleanup of the waterfront of the Golden Horn and the construction of an embankment; introduction of modern transportation systems such as regular steamboat and horse-drawn tram services, the subway between Galata and Pera, and the railroad; and construction of two bridges, Galata and Unkapanı, over the Golden Horn.[14] The south and the north of the Galata Bridge, Eminönü/Sirkeci and Karaköy, became the intersection points of the modern transportation systems and thus important focal points of the city from the nineteenth century on. Because of the lack of a comprehensive urban vision[15] and of investment, however, these piecemeal interventions could not bring back the good old days or make Istanbul one of the glorious modern capital cities of the nineteenth century. Nevertheless, they were effective in gathering the isolated parts of the city into a sort of fragmentary whole.

Even these insufficient modernization attempts lost momentum after the declaration of the new capital of the republic in 1923: Ankara. All energy and emotional and financial investments were allocated to Ankara until the 1950s.[16] At the same time, Istanbul also lost part of its non-Muslim population, the real generator of the urban economy. The 1920s were stagnation years for the city, and the rebuilding of Beyazıt Square on the site of the Byzantine Forum Tauri was the most significant urban development. In 1933, four well-known city planners, H. Prost, H. Elgoetz, A. Agache, and H. Lambert were invited to address the planning of the city. Among the three proposals (Prost did not participate in the competition), Elgoetz's was accepted as a guide for future developments. It was modest, concentrating on overcoming the dilapidation of the peninsula; the urban developments he envisioned were mainly restricted to attempts at regularization and sanitation.[17] He followed the period's prevailing tendencies in relation to the historical peninsula: cleaning up the immediate context of monuments and the historical center by decentralizating industry and displacing the harbor to Haydarpaşa and Yenikapı. He proposed to build four bridges over the Golden Horn and add the connections necessary to incorporate them with the existing network, to allocate the slopes along the shore to business and commercial centers, and to endow the waterfront with urban parks between the quays. For unclear reasons, however, his proposal was not implemented.

In 1936, H. Prost was installed as the city planner, and he remained in this position until 1950.[18] He concentrated on the redefinition of the city on the basis of land-use and functional zoning, but did not properly consider growth—the most critical aspect of modern planning. Because of his particular interest in Byzantine culture, the old Acropolis was classified as an archeological site. Like most of his contemporaries, he was obsessed with regularization and sanitation, and thus with cleaning up the immediate context of the monuments: Eminönü Square around Yenicami and Beyazıt Square, among others. Another proposal related to this ideal was the displacement of the harbor to Yenikapı and the expansion of the Galata harbor to save Sarayburnu, "one of the world's most beautiful views," from the "contamination" of the harbor. As an extension of this proposal, Atatürk

Boulevard connecting Unkapanı to Yenikapı and Aksaray Square were built, but the proposal itself was not implemented. His idea of connecting Europe to Asia with a bridge or a tunnel had to wait until the 1970s. Since his conservation agenda was limited to the conservation of image, his main concern was to preserve the silhouette of the peninsula by restricting building heights. Yet, as Heidegger pointed out, what ought to be preserved is the true nature of the context, that is, the restoration of the invisible. Thus in spite of his obsession with preservation, his applications lead to the deterioration of the generative nucleus of the city: the Golden Horn. Among his numerous implementations, the one that deeply influenced the Golden Horn was his insistence on functional zoning and the allocation of the west of the Unkapanı (Atatürk) Bridge to industry. The decision to concentrate industry around the Golden Horn condemned the vicinity to being the setting of environmental pollution and poverty until the 1980s.

In 1950 came another juncture in the history of modern Turkey. A. Menderes came to power in the election of 1950 by advocating liberal policies. He promoted the prosperity of Istanbul, the city of industry and commerce, as opposed to Ankara, the capital city. His idea of prosperity was based on regularization and sanitation. The 1950s were also the beginning of rapid urbanization and land speculation. The new urban model did not favor mass transportation but the private automobile and the detached apartment block (*apartman*). Accordingly, Menderes was eager to open up wide boulevards, even on the historical peninsula and Galata: Vatan Caddesi and Millet Caddesi in Aksaray are the well-known examples imposed blindly on the historical fabric of the city, and in Aksaray Square, on the site of Forum Bovis, a very complicated traffic junction was built. For the sake of these new arteries, the persistent city plan was effaced, the almost 3,000-year-old urban traces perished, and even the monuments were demolished. The brutality of his act was reminiscent of that of Haussmann, *artiste démolisseur,* but Menderes had no urban vision for building an equally powerful environment. These new arteries have no precedent in the collective memory of the city; they follow neither topography nor traces of the persistent urban structure. Thus the city has never internalized them; they have been unaccommodated elements of the city since then.

Istanbul had not developed any strategy to cope with rapid urbanization when it was hit by a migration wave in the 1950s. As an industrial zone, the

Golden Horn was an appropriate place for newcomers to settle and was soon invaded by squatters. Industry and squatters, the most violent aspects of modern urbanization, had covered the generative nucleus that the city had neglected until the 1980s.

THE REGENERATION OF THE GOLDEN HORN AFTER THE 1980s

The invasion of industry brought forth the dissolution of the heterogeneous, multilayered, multicultural configuration of the Golden Horn. Especially since 1950, the Golden Horn has drawn attention only because of the urban woes it hosted: pollution and poverty. The city began to view it as a backyard in which to hide what it does not want to confront.

In the mid-1980s, Mayor Bedrettin Dalan initiated a decentralization project to move industry to the periphery of the city, clean up the waterfront, and purify the sea. Dalan's interventions were daring but one-dimensional. They were motivated by his obsession with purification and sanitation and his desire for a homogeneous environment without contamination. Yet the operation fulfilled most of its objectives: water has been purified to a great extent, most of the industrial companies have left the Golden Horn (at most 10 factories are active today out of 151 in the nineteenth century[19]), and most of the industrial buildings have been demolished. On the other hand, the most important evidence of the history of modernization should have been documented before "cleaning up": the haphazard restoration of the waterfront caused irretrievable loss of industrial heritage. Reminiscent of the Elgoetz proposal, the resultant empty spaces along the shore have been converted into urban parks. Yet because there is no urban vision behind the operation, no grand project to rebuild, no creative intuition to inspire, the parks remain as bland green areas: they look like camouflage disguising the brutal act perpetrated there.[20] In urban interventions in a historical context, the appeal always derives from the dialectical relation between destruction and creativity. Destruction is inevitable to make room for the new; the new, however, should include both continuity and rupture, it should be intrinsically ambivalent in terms of its relation to the past. Without this ambivalence, urban intervention becomes pure violation. Thus in spite of the partial success in decentralization and sanitation, the overall intervention has left the waterfront as a desolate no-man's land for almost ten years.

In the 1990s, the remaining abandoned industrial buildings began to attract the attention of those who were developing projects to enhance the public realm of the city—projects such as museums, universities, cultural centers, and amusement parks. Apart from their architectural grandeur, their central position in the city with a promising waterfront inspired visionary people and nongovernmental organizations to set in motion their public projects.

In Karaköy, the warehouses and offices of the Maritime Enterprise, designed by S. H. Eldem in the 1950s, were abandoned in the 1980s because of the introduction of container-type transportation. Although the Passenger Terminal is still in use, the Mariner Freight Terminal was moved to Haydarpaşa. In 2004, one of the abandoned warehouses was converted into a temporary museum, Istanbul Modern, by Tabanlıoğlu Architects. A limited budget for the conversion meant a limited intervention. Within this framework, Tabanlıoğlu decided to use the basic nature of the warehouse: empty space, the most desirable quality for contemporary museums. Moreover, in this case, this convenient emptiness stands just across the most beautiful view of the city: the silhouette of the historical peninsula.

The Rahmi Koç Industrial Museum is one of the first renovation projects on the Golden Horn. The Ottoman Navy anchor factory *Lengerhane* and the Hasköy Shipyard were converted into a museum. The former was built in the eighteenth century over the foundation of a Byzantine building, and its renovation was completed in 1994; the latter was founded in 1861 and renovated in 2001. They both house Rahmi Koç's private collection of industrial products and machinery.

The renovation of the Silahtarağa power plant is the most recent project on the Golden Horn. With its 35,000 square meters of building area located on 118,000 square meters of land, it is also the most extensive. This was the first large-scale thermoelectric generator of the Ottoman Empire. It was built in 1913 by Ganz Electric Company of Hungary and closed in 1983. As the first power plant of Istanbul, its leading role in the modernization of the city is undeniable. Thus it is a marker not only of the industrial heritage but also of the social history of the city. It is a typical nineteenth-century industrial settlement with its production units, offices, different types of housing, and recreation facilities. With the overall conception of the settlement and its various formal articulations manifesting both local and universal attitudes of the

Notes
1. Cited in D. Kuban, *Istanbul, An Urban History: Byzantion, Constantinopolis, Istanbul* (Istanbul: Economic and Social Foundation of Turkey, 1996), p. 1.
2. Ibid., p.3
3. Cited in Z. Çelik, *The Remaking of Istanbul: Portrait of an Ottoman City in the Nineteenth Century* (Berkeley: University of California Press, 1986), p. 155.
4. In classical Greek, the suffix "ion" was used to denote the place; therefore "Byzantion" was "the place of Byzas."
5. Çelik, *The Remaking of Istanbul*, p. 11.
6. A. Rossi, in his book *The Architecture of the City*, stressed that the propelling permanence of the city comes from persistence of its overall plan and its monuments.
7. W. Müller-Wiener argued that instead of the traditional Roman grid plan, Constantine imagined a particular design for his new capital. This can be conceived as the self-realization of the city. See W. Müller-Wiener, *Istanbul'un Tarihsel Topografyası: 17. Yüzyıl Başlarına Kadar Byzantion-Konstantinopolis-Istanbul*, translated by Ü. Sayın (Istanbul: YKY, 2001), p. 19.
8. Ibid., p. 26.
9. Ibid., p. 29. Çelik gives the outcomes of the 1477 and 1535 censuses in which the ratios remain almost the same: Muslims constituted 58 percent, Christians 32 percent, and Jews 10 percent. In the late nineteenth century, the ratios change only slightly with Muslims still forming 55 percent of the total population. Çelik, *The Remaking of Istanbul*, p. 26.
10. Ortaylı calls the Ottoman Empire the third Roman Empire.
11. A *külliye* is a pious foundation system used as a strategy to trigger and at the same time control urbanization. It is a constituent element of the dwelling culture of the Ottomans and can be better understood by remembering that it was an Islamic society originating in Anatolia. This framework defined the relationship between Man/Nature/Object and also between private and public realms.
12. The pattern initiated by the Byzantines was maintained by the Ottomans (i.e., a chain of specialized commercial quays for fish, butter, firewood, fruit, wheat, etc., along the shores and their corresponding gates on the walls).
13. E. Yücetürk, *Haliç: Siluetin Oluşum-Değişim Süreci* (Istanbul: Haliç Belediyeler Birliği Yayınları, 2001), p. 78.
14. See Çelik, *The Remaking of Istanbul*, pp. 49–103.
15. Three proposals for the urban planning of Istanbul were designed during the first westernization attempts of the Ottoman empire: Von Moltke's (1839), Arnodin's (1900), and Bouvard's (1902). Von Moltke's proposal was significant for its resurfacing of the Byzantine

period, Silahtarağa also makes a particular case for the urban and technological developments of the European context. In 2003, Istanbul Bilgi University developed a comprehensive project to reanimate the whole settlement, not only in terms of the scale of architectural intervention but also in the scope of the program, subtly expressed by the name of the prospective complex: Santral Istanbul. In Turkish *santral* means center of distribution, source of power. Thus the name is reminiscent of the past, the previous function of the complex (power plant), and at the same time implies the future: a generator triggering latent creative energies among the different layers of society. It is to be a sociocultural as well as architectural regeneration.

The Sütlüce slaughterhouse was built in 1923 and demolished in the 1980s operation. It was designed in the "first national style." Nowadays an awkward enlarged replica is being erected on the same site. It can be used as a paradigmatic case of a fantasy-based intervention.

The Feshane textile factory has been an ill-fated building complex. It was built in 1833 and almost ruined in the fire of 1866, then rebuilt in the same place. It was enlarged and renovated in 1868 and 1916, and demolished in the 1980s except for the big hall built with prefabricated units. Since then, it has been subjected to various restoration attempts. Each has demonstrated the fact that restoration can cause irretrievable damage: sometimes a decent disappearance might be more fortunate for both the building and collective memory.

There is an ongoing rehabilitation program in the Fener-Balat district, a joint program of the European Union and the Fatih municipality that began in January 2003 and will end in October 2006. The program has four objectives: restoration of the houses, social rehabilitation, renovation of the historical Balat Market, and establishment of a waste management strategy.[21] Although the program stresses the importance of the active participation of inhabitants, this has not been achieved yet. In the beginning, homeowners were hesitant to accept grants offered for restoration of their houses because of conspiracy theories.[22] Nevertheless, as they see accomplishments in their neighborhood, they begin to be more enthusiastic about cooperation—ironically, toward the end of the project. At any rate, it is obvious that gentrification will be a serious issue for the whole vicinity, making it important to develop preventive strategies. It is also crucial to call attention to the fact that regeneration of a district is not merely an aesthetic issue; it is an existential problem for the city itself, affecting the preservation of its vitality.

Cibali Tobacco Factory was designed by Vallaury in the 1880s and abandoned in 1995. In 1997, it was transferred to Kadir Has University. Its restoration began in 2000 and was completed in 2001. It is a careful restoration based on cleaning up and repairing. The university was awarded the European Union Prize for Cultural Heritage in 2003 (European Nostra Award).

Recently, the reconstruction of Eminönü-Sirekeci as an urban public space has been on the municipal agenda. The district had accommodated the harbor from the beginning until the 1950s, making it attractive to different cultures, particularly during the Byzantine period. As the commercial center of the city, it was embellished with impressive monuments during the Ottoman empire: Yeni Camii (New Mosque), Rüstem Paşa Mosque, Tahtakale Hamamı (public bath), Mısır Çarşısı, and other large commercial buildings (hans). It was one of the most important harbors of the world and therefore has always been one of the most active districts of the city. Yet with the construction of the bridge between Eminönü and Galata and the introduction of modern transportation systems, it became the intersection of these systems, and activity intensified starting in the mid-nineteenth century. During the Republican period, especially when Lütfi Kırdar was governor and mayor of the city (1938–49), as a result of the obsessive attempts at regularization and sanitation, the immediate contexts of the monuments were clarified and Eminönü Square was opened. During Menderes' operation (1955–56), the fish market was demolished because of the construction of the Unkapanı-Eminönü road. Then came Dalan's operation in the 1980s, destroying the Yemiş wharf and its surroundings and "cleaning up" the waterfront (except for Zindan Han, Ahi Çelebi Mosque, Değirmen Han, and a small part of the city walls).[23] These operations also "cleaned up" the very spirit of the district, reducing it to a mere traffic junction since then. The municipality now seems determined to reconstruct the district. There is no comprehensive project yet, but some studies have been carried out.

skeleton: the five main arteries extending from east to west and connecting the city center to the city gates endowed the peninsula with a sense of regularity, but they did need the connections on the southwest axis to form an uninterrupted modern network extending infinitely and to define a structural whole. He also stressed the conversion of wooden construction to masonry. With emphasis on regularity, Von Moltke's proposal shed light for subsequent urban interventions on the peninsula, but it was a corrective scheme rather than a visionary one offering a fresh image of a modern city.

Arnodin's proposal, on the other hand, was based on a new ring road, which was in fact part of a broader scheme for connecting Europe to Asia. The ring would define the metropolitan area and directions for possible growth. As such, it encouraged growth and change, rather than preserving the existing context. But because it required radical change and thus needed serious engagement and considerable investment, it failed to get government support.

Bouvard's proposal was based on images of a Baroque city. Yet because they were just pictorial drafts, the most critical point of the so-called plan was that there was no hint as to the interrelation between these partial sketches or their relation to the topography. As such they were impressive but impractical. See Çelik, The Remaking of Istanbul, pp. 104–125.

16. The poet Yahya Kemal described the problem of Istanbul in those days: "Istanbul has so far lived on consumption, now it has to live on production." From Ilhan Tekeli, The Development of the Istanbul Metropolitan Area: Urban Administration and Planning (Istanbul: IULA-EMME and Yıldız Technical University, 1994), p. 68.

17. See Kuban, Istanbul: An Urban History, pp. 418–419, Tekeli, The Development of the Istanbul Metropolitan Area, pp. 76–77, and Yücetürk, Haliç: Siluetin Oluşum-Değişim Süreci, p. 96.

18. See Kuban, Istanbul: An Urban History, pp. 419–423, Tekeli, The Development of the Istanbul Metropolitan Area, pp. 77–88, and Yücetürk, Haliç: Siluetin Oluşum-Değişim Süreci, pp. 97–98.

19. T. G. Köksal and H. H. Kargın, "Haliç'teki Endüstri Mirasının Geçmişi ve Geleceği," in Dünü ve Bugünü ile Haliç: Sempozyum Bildirileri 22–23 Mayıs 2003 (Istanbul: Kadir Has Üniversitesi, 2004), p. 431.

20. The operation is reminiscent of the "destructive character" cited by Walter Benjamin.

21. See: http://fenerbalat.org/

22. This lack of confidence shows how the deteriorated district is not just an aesthetic problem.

23. See Z. Çelik, "Eminönü," Istanbul in the Insurance Maps of Jacques Pervititich (Istanbul: Axa Oyak), p. 133.

PARS KIBARER

SIRKECI SQUARE: The Evolution of a Transient Space

SIRKECI SQUARE

Under the dramatic skyline of Istanbul sits Sirkeci, known to many as a bustling business district. Situated on the north of the historical peninsula between Eminönü and Sarayburnu, it is part of a commercial hub that centers around Eminönü and stretches toward Unkapanı. Nearby are Topkapı, the royal palace of the Ottoman sultan, Gülhane public gardens, the governor's office, and nineteenth-century inns. Sirkeci is a transition point for many who arrive in the historic city. It is most notable as the railway terminus on the European side of Istanbul, the counterpart of which is Haydarpaşa on the Asian side. The waterfront of Sirkeci is lined with piers that accommodate passenger and car ferries crossing the Bosphorus. Trams cut through Sirkeci before the station to make their way to the square in Sultanahmet and on to their final destinations.

A chaotic atmosphere prevails in Sirkeci. The disarrayed, almost organic accumulation of some functions and absence of others suggests the necessity to reconsider the area both functionally and aesthetically. A new development is going to add to the confluence of services and functions in the near future: a subway tunnel, part of a massive commuter-rail project, will cross the Bosphorus under the sea to channel thousands of commuters to and from the historic peninsula. An underground station will be located in Sirkeci. With the addition of this project, the intensification of the area's current state as a transition point is bound to exacerbate the problematic circumstances. Nevertheless, the evident conditions of Sirkeci set a stage for an interactive space, one that is not yet completely defined and comprehensively organized.

01 Sirkeci Square after the cleaning up of old buildings in front of the station toward the Ankara Avenue in the 1930's. (Photo: Selahattin Giz, Yapı Kredi Collection)

EARLY DEVELOPMENT

In Istanbul, it is hard not to refer to history even when discussing the emergence of new models in the city. The rich historical layering compels one to look back into the past to better understand spatial development. Given its primary location at the mouth of the Golden Horn, Sirkeci has evolved through the years to acquire its distinctive attributes as a node. In Byzantine times, it was a significant harbor known as Prosphorianos. During the Ottoman period, this area served as the port and customs point of the empire, engendering activity and development. In the second half of the nineteenth century, given the presence of the port, the trains were brought to Sirkeci to link the maritime activities and the railroad. This historical move concentrated the already dense urban core, creating a complicated knot still present today.

Urban transformation in Istanbul began mainly as a result of political changes in the Ottoman Empire, most notably the 1839 Tanzimat Decree, a set of military, educational, and administrative reforms made by Sultan Abdülmecit (1839-61). The period following Tanzimat could be seen as the period of Westernization, with visible consequences in the built environment of the capital city of Istanbul. In this period, the city's development was driven by the establishment of new political offices and the reorganization of existing ones (e.g., the creation of Nafia Nezareti, the ministry of reconstruction, in 1849, and of şehremaneti, the municipal council, in 1955). The impacts of these changes were felt in the provision of new infrastructure such as streets, sidewalks, street lighting, squares, sewers, and drains, which began to transform the Ottoman capital into a modern metropolis.[1] An extensive building campaign of palaces, mosques, and institutions was undertaken. With the help of foreign investors and entrepreneurs, transportation networks in the city started to take shape.

Railroad transport was found indispensable for the economic, military, and political advantages it promised. It was important in the unification of the empire, leading to control over the Balkans. The railroad would physically connect the capital to Europe and engender direct communication. It would also allow Ottomans to control commercial activities. In this respect, initiatives were taken as early as 1856. After three unsuccessful contracts, the final concession for building and operating the railroad was granted to a Belgian banker, Baron Maurice de Hirsch, in 1969.[2] Hirsch started operations under the name Rumeli Railroad Company.

Initially the railroad was laid only between Küçükçekmece and Yedikule, linking the suburban districts, and ending where the city walls began. Discontinuing the railroad at the gates of city walls was a common practice, witnessed in a number of European cities such as Paris and Vienna, but in Istanbul the great distance between the center and the walls was found ineffi-cient for the transport of people and goods. Bringing the rail-road to Sirkeci was at first a confounding problem, but it was in fact easily resolved. Despite the resistance of bureaucrats and esteemed officials of the time, and disregarding alternative solutions for arrival in the city, Sultan Abdülaziz (1861–76) approved the laying of train tracks by the walls of Topkapı Palace, even at the cost of tearing down palatial buildings.[3] His tolerant attitude might reflect the lost preeminence of Topkapı Palace in the sultan's eyes; in 1856 he had left Topkapı for a new royal residence, Dolmabahçe, located on the banks of Bosphorus outside the historic city.

02 The building which occupied the corner of Sirkeci Square has been demolished during the construction of the Kennedy Highway. (Photo: Selahattin Giz, Yapı Kredi Collection)

The railroad from Sirkeci-Yedikule and Küçükçekmece-Çatalca was opened in July 1872 and extended to Edirne the following year.[4] At first a small building functioned as a train station in Sirkeci. This building is still in place, but abandoned today. Within a year of this building's opening, another proj-ect was presented to Sultan Abdülaziz, consisting of a new train station and ancillary facilities. Another project drawn at the request of Esat Paşa, the grand vizier of the time, was comparatively larger and included a wharf and warehouses.[5] Although the latter project provided a more comprehensive solu-tion to the site, given the financial constraints of the time, the initial project was given a start. During a sixteen-year project delay, Abdülhamit II (1876–1909) was enthroned as sultan; he was keen on continuing Abdülaziz's railroad operation.

Architect August Carl Friedrich Jasmund, a graduate of the Berlin Koniglich Bauakamedie, was chosen to design the train station. According to records, Jasmund had left his position in Berlin, at the ministry of public works, to visit the Ottoman Empire to study orientalist architecture.[6] He visit-ed Manisa, Edirne, and Bursa, as well as other small towns, and stayed in Istanbul after he was offered commissions by the Ottoman Empire. In 1888, he was asked by the Rumeli Railroad Company to design the Sirkeci train sta-tion, which was realized in next three years.

The station's ornate orientalist design can be regarded as a symbol of an association with the West and the station's role as gateway to Europe. Orientalism, an eclectic style invented by Westerners to evoke an exotic image of the East, was deemed appropriate for welcoming Europeans to the capital.

(The first journey of the famous Orient Express was made in 1883, predating the station. Departing from the Gare de l'Est in Paris, it made stops at Strasbourg, Karlsruhe, Stuttgart, Ulm, Munich, Vienna, Budapest, Bucharest, and Varna before arriving in Sirkeci.[7])

03 Aerial view of Sirkeci and Sarayburnu before Kennedy Highway and the Florya coastal road were built. (Photo: Selahattin Giz, Yapı Kredi Collection)

The most important factor related to bringing trains to Sirkeci is the existence of the harbor. At mid-century, the harbor was inadequate for loading, unloading, and storing; its improvement was an economic and military necessity. In the Paris Treaty of 1856 following the Crimean War, the poor conditions were addressed by the French and English, who wanted to expand their trade network over the empire.[8] Lighthouses and ports were considered imperative. During the war against Russia, the empire's allies, France and England, had sent military equipment, but much difficulty was encountered during disembarkation. Although lighthouses were built immediately after the treaty, the building of the quays was a venture that was postponed until 1879. Marius Michel, a French captain, took on the responsibility of expanding the ports, a grueling and risky undertaking. The project saw delays, but in 1892 building began on the banks of Tophane on the Galata side.[9] The Sirkeci side was started in 1894. A number of filling operations were unsuccessful because of the depth of the water and the muddy seabed. After several foiled attempts, the Sirkeci side was finally finished in 1900, costing nine times the initial estimate.[10]

Public transportation by sea before the introduction of steamboats was facilitated by rowboats or sailboats operating between the shores of the Bosphorus. In 1828 a steamboat was presented to the sultan as a gift, and more boats were acquired in the following years. A shipyard was opened to build steamboats, and in later years the Golden Horn became a suitable location for the expansion of this industry. Initially Russian and English companies provided transportation services by sea along the Bosphorus. The first transportation company owned by the government was Fervaid-i Osmaniye, but this company operated on a limited basis.[11] In 1851, Şirket-i Hayriye was established to provide sea transportation across the Bosphorus and Marmara as well as to more distant destinations. Sirkeci was an important drop-off location. From here trips were made to Princes' Islands, Pendik, and Yesilkoy. The world's first car ferry was chartered in Istanbul in 1872. The earliest trips were made between Üsküdar and Sirkeci, and Üsküdar and Kabataş.

URBAN INTERVENTIONS

In the eighty-two-year history of the modern republic, a large number of urban interventions were carried out that affected the micro and macro form of the city. In speaking about Sirkeci proper, however, urban interventions guided by French planner Henri Prost and "honorary mayor" Adnan Menderes can be singled out, as their localized approaches were particularly influential in shaping this area.

The reconstruction operations undertaken during the mandate of mayor and governor Lütfi Kırdar (1939–48) are attributed to the Istanbul master plans signed by Prost. Under Prost's supervision, significant planning activities were carried out between 1936 and 1950. Although the plans were widely criticized at the time of completion and not fully implemented given the start of World War II, much of the city's present appearance can be credited to these plans. The transportation network envisioned by Prost makes up the backbone of the system today.

In 1933, Prost was invited to enter a competition involving three other experts—German Herman Elgoetz and French Alfred Agache and Jack H. Lambert—yet Prost was not able to enter.[12] Elgoetz won the competition, but his winning entry was not implemented. In 1936, Prost arrived in Istanbul in response to President Mustafa Kemal Atatürk's invitation to participate in the planning of that city. From the start, Prost emphasized the importance of protecting the historic urban legacy. Nevertheless, he proposed to equip the urban environment with the technological means necessary to modernize the city. The first plan, in 1/5,000 scale, was completed in 1937 and approved in 1939. In this plan, roads were devised to keep expropriation to a minimum in relation to the new tunnels, bridges, and viaducts required by the shifting urban topography. The plan also aimed at unifying the city with a transportation network of trams, railways, and ferries, and arranging inner-city traffic to facilitate easy movement.[13]

04 Aerial photo showing the storage facilities that occupied the stretch between Sirkeci and Eminönü. (Photo: Selahattin Giz, Yapı Kredi Collection)

One of the most important planning rules introduced by Prost was the establishment of a height restriction in the historical peninsula: no building could rise above 12 meters in height on land 40 meters above sea level in the historical peninsula. This rule is still enforced today, to control the silhouette of the city. The most unsatisfactory aspect of Prost's plan, however, was siting industrial quarters on the banks of Haliç. This decision can be traced to Prost's aesthetic interest in concealing industry in Haliç to maintain the scenic beauty of the Bosphorus. Yet this placement caused much damage, and the consequences remain problematic for the city.

Many important public squares and parks of Istanbul were established according to Prost plans, including Maçka Park (Demokrasi Park) and Taksim Gezisi (İnönü Gezisi). Buildings surrounding important monuments or occupying vital centers were cleared. Along with Eminönü and Beyazıt Squares, Sirkeci was opened up by the removal of buildings to create a spacious location for the tram station. The area was improved by the addition of sidewalks and planting. Ankara Street, which leads to Cağaloğlu, was asphalted. As mentioned in the plan notes, Prost firmly opposed keeping the port in its present location in Sirkeci.[14] As industry and trade grew wider, the limited space would not allow the expansion necessary for ancillary facilities. Railroad transportation was already losing prominence, as trucking was becoming more widely accepted.

Another disconcerting situation for Prost was the isolation of the park in Sarayburnu from public use. Prost proposed connecting the Galata Bridge and the park with a promenade shaded with trees, reserved for the residents of the Istanbul. Prost advised moving the port to Yenikapı, as this was the most appropriate location for this facility. From Yenikapı, ferries could directly load and unload cargo and make easy trips to Haydarpaşa. Only electrified trains carrying passengers from suburban lines would reach Sirkeci, and the part of the railroad from Yenikapı to Sirkeci could then be replaced

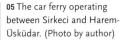

05 The car ferry operating between Sirkeci and Harem-Üsküdar. (Photo by author)

06 Üsküdar pier, one of the piers along the coast between Sirkeci and Eminönü, and Karaköy, on the other side of the coast. (Photo by author)

07 Kennedy Highway opened during mandate of Prime Minister Adnan Menderes.(Photo by author)

by a boulevard.[15] If the port stayed, Prost recommended a high boardwalk, as in Antwerp and Algiers.

A project from 1941 drawn up by Prost for Sirkeci might hint at what he meant. This project describes a double-tier organization, with the road extending from Eminönü lifted to arrive at the upper level. This level serves as a drop-off platform with parking and waiting areas, a restaurant, a coffee-house, and storage units. From the platform, passengers can also access the ships. The road continues and ramps down toward Sarayburnu to arrive at the car-ferry terminal. The lower level serves as a loading and unloading plat-form, with access to cargo trains. The multifunctional character of this proj-ect is highly interesting, as it pragmatically solves the problem of the port by separating functions into two levels while connecting to Sarayburnu and the curving road parallel to the train tracks. This project was not carried out, however, and Prost's suggestions concerning the port in Yenikapı were found unviable by other authorities.

08 The main entrance to the Sirkeci Train Station as devised by Auguste Jasmund. Today, however, passengers use the side entry as the main entrance to the station. (Photo by author)

Postwar developments in Istanbul greatly altered the form of the city. Illegal housing became a huge problem. Thousands of migrants from rural lands started to pour into the city and settle on the periphery. An increase in the subdivision of land outside of municipal boundaries, and related residen-tial development, and an acceleration of industrialization accompanied by the need for factory sites forced the city to expand.[16] Ignoring socio-economic problems, Adnan Menderes sponsored a great urban clearing that conformed to a political agenda. With the advantage of new laws that facilitated less cost-ly expropriation, he began a massive demolition and development campaign in the city, starting in 1956. In the next three and a half years, 7,289 buildings were appropriated, compared to only 1,148 buildings taken during the tenure of Lütfi Kırdar.[17]

Prost had left his post at the end of 1950. In 1951–52, a commission was formed to revise the Prost plan; several members of this commission were later chosen to serve as members of a board of consultants, to handle plan-ning activities with the municipality. In early 1957, German Hans Högg was hired and immediately started preparing plans. However, these plans merely provided rationalizations for Menderes's already determined undertakings.[18] The operations were focused on the historic peninsula and destroyed many historic buildings to create large boulevards and squares, threatening the spatial character of the Ottoman fabric. For instance, Vatan and Millet

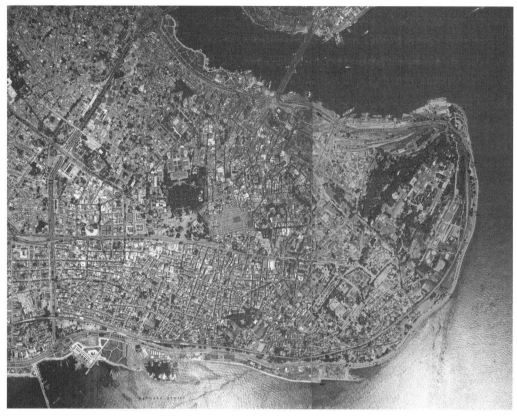

09 Aerial view of the historical peninsula. (Photo: Istanbul
Greater Municipality Maps Department)

10 Aerial view of Sirkeci in close-up. (Photo: Istanbul
Greater Municipality Maps Department)

Boulevards were opened, Atatürk Boulevard was widened, and an elaborate intersection was created in Aksaray.

The interventions specifically related to Sirkeci were the widening of Ankara Avenue and the establishment of the Sirkeci-Florya coastal road. These two interventions aimed to relieve heavy traffic congestion in Sirkeci and Eminönü. Ankara Avenue, which ramps up to the governor's office and Cağaloğlu, was enlarged to 20m.[19] The street known today as Ragıp Gümüş Pala Avenue extended from Eminönü to lead toward Ankara Avenue, curved in front of the station, and came to a dead end in Gülhane. The road known today as Kennedy Highway was opened up as an extension of Ragıp Gümüş Pala Avenue and continued around the tip of the peninsula, cutting through land owned by the Directory of Railways. Kennedy Highway runs 22km to Florya, parallel to the city walls until Yedikule, creating an alternative scenic road to the London highway that travels through the inner land. Earlier, the railroad and the walls created a strong edge, whereas the opening of this road physically connected people with the sea.

As described by Doğan Kuban, a considerable difference lies between the urban images these two approaches were aiming to create.[20] The early interventions during Lütfi Kırdar under the supervision of Prost were geared toward designing public spaces for the citizens of Istanbul. In this period, reflecting the early republic's social and cultural policies, historical monuments were opened to public visits, public squares and parks were created, and public transportation was the mode that connected the city. Menderes's

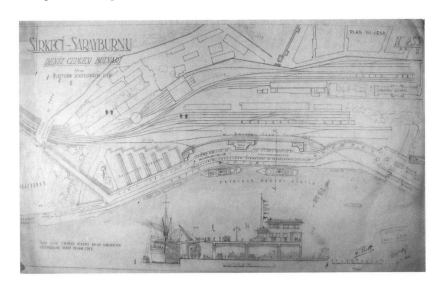

11 Proposal by Henri Prost for Sirkeci and Sarayburnu. (Property of Istanbul Atatürk Kitaplığı.)

12 Panoramic view of Sirkeci.
(Photo by author)

operations, conversely, were more about changing the image to that of a modern city accessible by car, in tune with modernist precepts. In the years that followed, Istanbul's population grew exponentially, almost justifying the scale of activities during the Menderes reconstruction period and even rendering those broad interventions inadequate.

PRESENT CONDITION Planning activities following the Menderes operation approached the urban environment in a broader way, considering the city as a whole rather than in fragments. Threats to the urban environment were discussed and studied in relation to their economic and social underpinnings. Urban squatters and housing topped the list, followed by transportation and the relocation of industry and related activities. In these years, however, no significant operations can be singled out that relate to the reconsideration or establishment of public squares in Istanbul with coordinated policies on public space. The squares of Istanbul became transportation or transition nodes cramped by buses, taxis, cars, and sometimes trams, resulting in polluted, loud, chaotic, and overall unpleasant places lacking in urban quality.

Sirkeci's current situation is no different, and in fact, it is in some ways worse than other squares of Istanbul. The train station, once a symbolic marker of the Square, a celebration of trains arriving in Istanbul, can now

hardly be recognized as a significant architectural monument. The dilapidat-
ed condition of the station and the empty ancillary facilities signals the lack
of concern given to railways in Turkey. Similar undesirable circumstances can
also be observed in Haydarpaşa. For both public transportation and shipping, there has been a gradual decline in use of trains, largely because of the
flexible operations provided by trucks and buses with the establishment of an
extensive highway network throughout the country. Based on transportation
policies developed by the government, investment in railroads has been very
limited since late 1950s. As a result, the railroad network has been enlarged
by only 11 percent, while the highway network has been increased by about 80
percent in the same period. Trains provide 2 percent of public transportation
and only 4 percent of total freight transportation. Freight trains that come
from the West now stop in Kapıkule and do not enter the heart of the city.
Passenger trains, however, operate between Halkalı and Sirkeci. These trains
tend to serve lower-income groups arriving in the city from peripheral locations and poor neighborhoods.

   The railway directory is currently renting out the area surrounding the
station as a parking facility to generate income. The gas station located on the
grounds of the formal garden of the station not only blocks the monumental
building but serves as a roundabout for cars, generating constant traffic during the day. Abandoned repair docks, administrative offices, and the old train
station only add to the disharmony. On the waterfront, the piers and structures where one waits for ferries crossing the Bosphorus are all in disrepair.
These structures are also too small to accommodate the daily circulation of
people. There are also long lines for cars and buses waiting to enter the
grounds of the car-ferry terminal. Kennedy Highway, being a relatively fast
and wide thoroughfare, severs physical interaction between the waterfront

13 Panoramic view of the premises of the Station, currently
used as a parking facility.
(Photo by author)

and the inner areas of the urban fabric, and the substantial walls and fences of the closed-off railroad blocks the streets of Hocapaşa and brings them to a dead end. For crowds streaming to or from Ankara Avenue, one cumbersome overpass on the corner closer to Eminönü is clearly inadequate.

A new transportation project is under way to ameliorate the traffic problems of the city. Referred to as Marmaray, this project will extend a continuous railroad system between Halkalı on the European side and Gebze on the Asian side. Existing railroad tracks in both sides of the city will be connected by a subway tunnel under the Bosphorus. The tunnel is planned to go beneath the earth's surface in Kadıköy and first connect to Üsküdar Square, then it will cut across under the Bosphorus to arrive in Sirkeci, and finally emerge in Yedikule. As part of the project, Yenikapı is going to be developed to become an intermodal hub, as envisioned by Prost in the late 1930s. Ferries, trains, trams, and buses will intersect here, and a large parking complex will accommodate cars. According to estimates, the upgraded railway system will carry 75,000 passengers per hour, over seven times the current capacity of the system. To minimize the impact on historical buildings, and because of the difficulty of expropriation, the subway station in Sirkeci will be completely underground. There will be two entry-exit locations, one next to the current train station and the other bordering Ankara Avenue close to the governor's office. The ventilation towers will be concealed within the urban fabric of the Hocapaşa, a neighborhood behind the Sirkeci train station.

The area consisting of Eminönü, Cağaloğlu, Tahtakale, and Sirkeci is a major business center, attracting people from all around the city, and Sirkeci is the arrival point for many of these people. Urban interventions and urban dynamics are constantly redefining the character of enclaves of the city. In the early part of the century, Sirkeci was the thriving place for shipping and bus companies, storage facilities, cheap hotels, and restaurants. Migrants arrived here for work and stayed in these hotels in the vicinity of the station and the port. After the 1960s, Sirkeci lost some of its primacy as a service center with the removal of the port and new locations for buses. Bus companies were moved to a Thracian bus terminal in Topkapı, and transport companies were relocated to the periphery of the city in Zeytinburnu.[21] Yet Sirkeci today continues to exist as a business district and receives thousands of people. According to the Istanbul Chamber of Trade registrations, Sirkeci provides a significant marketplace for electronics, bus, truck, and automobile parts, photographic and cinematographic equipment, shipping companies and customs consultants, and optometric products. With the arrival of the subway tunnel, Sirkeci will most likely be redefined as a business center, prompting changes in the dynamics of the region.

The trend toward privatization is transforming the spaces of public life. Istanbul has developed into a series economically segregated regions, especially with the proliferation of housing developments as gated communities. Outsized shopping centers, now common in Istanbul, provide pseudo public spaces, as citizens are considered only as potential customers. The government is selling properties to generate income: Galataport, formerly the port and storage facility in Karaköy, has been sold to private companies to be developed into a hotel district. The grounds of the Hilton hotel, which were government property and part of the greenbelt that buffered the old city from new developments, were sold to a local investor, to develop when Hilton's contract expires. There are discussions about privatizing Haydarpaşa station; the building is slowly being vacated and may become a hotel in the near future.

There is definitely a change awaiting Sirkeci, and in fact a belated one. The railroad, which has been causing a knot in its current location, must be reconsidered, as port activity moved away from the site long ago. As in other European cities, the establishment of car-free streets and urban corridors has become highly popular in Istanbul, for these address the lack of accessible space in the city. The urban corridor of Istiklal has attracted people from all walks of life. The multilayered space with coffeehouses, bars, bookstores, and restaurants is full of people at all times. Officials are considering a similar strategy for Sirkeci, which might subtly improve conditions. However, Sirkeci deserves a much stronger intervention that can address both the site and the waterfront. Sensitive design and careful organization of the site in relation to urban dynamics can offer the value Sirkeci deserves and provide a place that is not merely a flexible transition point, but a place that can be joyfully inhabited. The site can become a place for small-scale experiences as well as grand civic events. In other words, given its place beneath the monuments and the remarkable skyline, Sirkeci could develop into a unique public space accessible and welcoming to both citizens and visitors of Istanbul.

Notes
1. Zeynep Çelik, *The Remaking of Istanbul: Portrait of an Ottoman City in the Nineteenth Century* (Berkeley: University of California Press, 1993), pp. 43–44.
2. Vahdettin Engin, *Rumeli Demiryolları* (Istanbul. Eren Yayıncılık, 1993), p. 49.
3. Ibid., pp. 69–70.
4. Ibid., pp. 108 and 117.
5. Mehmet Yavuz, "Mimar August Jasmund Hakkında Bilmediklerimiz." *Sanat Tarihi Dergisi* No. 8-1, April 2004, pp. 181–205.
6. Ibid.
7. However, the difficulty of passing through the Iron Curtain countries forced the Orient Express to stop running in 1977. In 1982, the Orient Express resumed its course, this time passing through London and Venice.
8. Eser Tutel. *Gemiler, Süvariler, İskeleler* (İletişim Yayınları. 1998), pp. 276–277.
9. Ibid., p. 282.
10. Ibid., p. 289.
11. Kuban, Doğan. *İstanbul Bir Kent Tarihi : Bizantion, Konstantinopolis, İstanbul.* Beşiktaş, İstanbul: Türkiye Ekonomik ve Toplumsal Tarih Vakfı, 1996), p. 359.
12. Ilhan Tekeli, *The Development of the Istanbul Metropolitan Area: Urban Planning and Administration* (IULA-EMME, Yıldız Technical University, 1994), p. 76.
13. Ibid., p. 87.
14. Henri Prost. "H. Prost'un Istanbul Nazım Planı Raporu Hakkında Notlar" (dated 1936), *Istanbul Araştırmaları 3.* Istanbul Kent Araştırmaları Merkezi. 1997.
15. Tekeli, p. 212.
16. Ibid., p. 103.
17. Ibid., p. 124.
18. Ibid., p. 121.
19. *İstanbul'un Kitabı.* İstanbul Vilâyeti Neşriyat ve Turizm Müdürlüğü. 1957.
20. Kuban, p. 395.
21. Tekeli, p. 221.

No metropolitan area displays as much face as Istanbul. Endless panoramas unfold along its streets and public squares. This condition of heightened visibility is made possible by the city's amazing geographic location along the Bosphorus between the European and Asian sides, and between the Marmara and Black Seas. This dramatic geography is further enhanced by three interlocking peninsulas across wide bodies of water and a soft hillscape that allows visibility deep into the interior of the city. Because of the constant need to cross the Bosphorus, by ferry or car, the citizens of Istanbul enjoy open vistas daily, though they also experience serious traffic problems that result from this constant crossing and the slowness of intermodal transportation. The arrival points by ferry at the bases of the bridges are usually large, informal open spaces that are loosely linked with each other and with other open spaces such as public gardens and the front yards of mosques; these arrival spaces provide at once adequate casualness for quick passage, scale for monumentality, and clearing for orientation.

In the past fifty years, the city population has increased from about 1 million to 15 million, and growth has expanded inland beyond the connection to the water and the views. Recent master plans have emphasized traffic planning: the most recent plan proposes, among other things, the creation of a multimodal 2-kilometer-long tunnel between the two continents under the Bosphorus. The tunnel has now been reduced to a train tunnel, a project being undertaken by a Japanese company. About one third of Istanbulis live on the Asian side. With 75,000 people crossing every hour, the flow of traffic in the city, between Asia and Europe, and the directions of Istanbul's growth will radically change. The technical work has been completed but the design work has yet to begin, and this is where we enter.

The first station for the tunnel on the European side will be in Sirkeci Square. The introduction of the tunnel station will no doubt radically alter the relationship

INTERMODAL ISTANBUL STUDIO:
SITE AND CONTEXT

between the existing modes of transportation and the use of the open spaces between them. It will also alter the perception of the city. This is the first time in the history of the city that citizens will cross the Bosphorus without seeing Istanbul.

The studio focused on the redesign of the Sirkeci Square area. The studio dealt mainly with the historic station building, the new station, the open space that accommodates the tram, the ferry terminal and the railyards, and the interspersed archeological sites. As elucidated in the essay by Pars Kibarer, the Square has always maintained an open play among these components. Ironically, it is the vastness of the area and its strategic location at the tip of the Golden Horn that has kept these pieces from aggregating into more than a sum of disparate parts. Each student explored different possibilities of intersection among these elements. They worked with the instruments of urban design, landscape, and architecture to decide, for example, whether the modes of transportation should converge on one major hub, intersect in pairs, or maintain separation; whether the open spaces should be unified or kept detached; and whether the surrounding blocks should be redeveloped—in sum, whether and how to synthesize across modes of transportation and scales of design.

The Square has always kept a rather informal aspect, verging on the illicit, and even if such activities reflect some of the space's vitality, it would be impossible to accept their formalization by design. Instead, the students studied the transient urban conditions that intermodality introduces as well as the spatial and social gaps, or blind spots, that always occur at the points of intersection between different networks. It is these aspects of public spaces that became the focus of their design inquiries, allowing for overall orchestration without overall control. As described by Tansel Korkmaz in her essay on the evolution of the Golden Horn, a better understanding of the limitations of design implementation could lead, as some of the projects have aimed to show, to an altogether different approach to design that operates within the possibilities offered by points of intersection within networks rather than by their overall control.

Whereas the visibility from the Square and the questions of interaction and interface are important in helping reorganize the city and its *meydans*, equally important is the way in which the Square is viewed from outside. It is rather humbling to design at the base of such a skyline (Topkapı, the Agia Sophia, and the Blue Mosque), but the tip of the peninsula, the most prominent moment in Istanbul, has always been a blind spot in the city. The challenge of the studio was to address this condition of invisibility, perhaps by thinking through a series of formal possibilities that emphasize the subliminal as a prelude to the sublime, that promote emptiness of public space as a necessity for full urban life, and that stretch the horizontality of its spatial disposition as a precondition for the eruption of a vibrant skyline. The studio dwelled on a potential for architecture that has yet to be fully explored, a skillful disappearing act that renders everything around it all the more visible.

CHRIS WHITE 132

DAVID BROWN 136

CHUNG-CHIEN CHIANG 140

KENSUKE SOEJIMA 142

JUSTINE KWIATKOWSKI 146

KOTCHAKORN VORAAKHOM 148

KRISTIN HOPKINS 150

NATALIE RINNE 152

OSCAR OLIVER 154

PHOEBE SCHENKER 156

SARAH HOLTON 158

THOMAS HUSSEY 160

AHMED KHADIER 164

INTERMODAL ISTANBUL STUDIO: STUDENT WORK

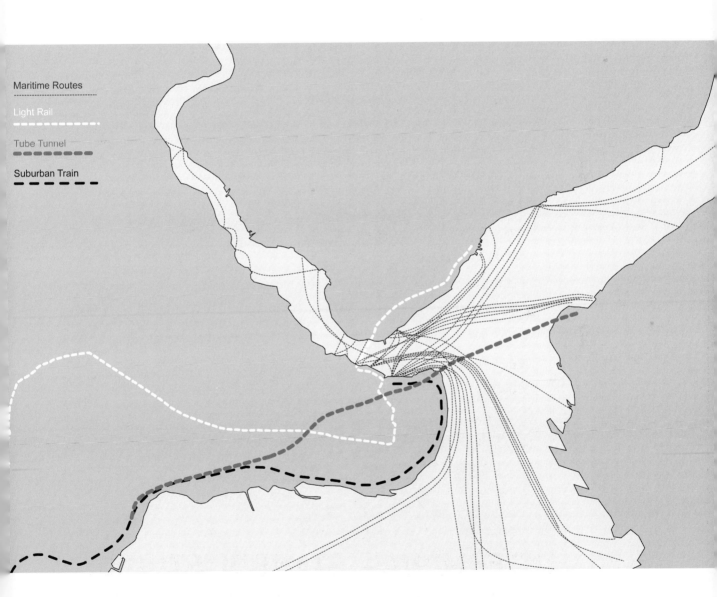

Maritime Routes

Light Rail

Tube Tunnel

Suburban Train

The infrastructure in Eminönü—the ferry terminals, the Kennedy Highway, the commuter train lines, and the informal parking areas—runs in bands parallel to the waterfront. These bands in the northeast corner of the Istanbul peninsula are disconnected from each other and the city both physically and visually.

The new subway—the Marmaray project—will run roughly parallel to these existing infrastructures, but underground. This change in section of infrastructure—the tunnel—offers a new method of crossing the existing bands of infrastructure and connects them via an underground passage. The current designs for the Marmaray project include point connections within the city fabric behind Sirkeci train station. Although these points connect the subway to the city fabric, the tram line, and Sirkeci Station, they ignore the possibility of connecting passengers to the waterfront, a place from which the city becomes visually evident.

This project aims to connect the Marmaray project directly to the ferry terminals in front of Sirkeci Station, and to redesign and unify the segment of waterfront that lies between the existing car-ferry depot and the international press building. The project recognizes that the waterfront in Eminönü is not continuous, but rather is separated into distinct segments. The redesign of this one segment of waterfront creates opportunities for improved physical connections between the various modes of transportation in and around Sirkeci Station, and for improved visual connections between the waterfront and the rest of

01

eminonu waterfront
relationships between waterfront/road/city

01 DIAGRAM 3: EMINONU WATERFRONT   The relationships between the water, Kennedy Highway, and Eminönü are defined by edge conditions that promote or deny connectivity. The language of these edge conditions is employed in the project to improve the legibility and fluidity of connections between the various modes of transportation converging on the site.

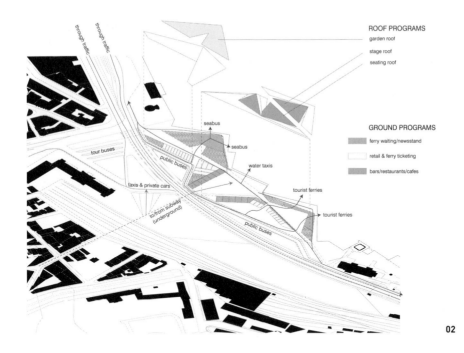

ROOF PROGRAMS
garden roof
stage roof
seating roof

GROUND PROGRAMS
ferry waiting/newsstand
retail & ferry ticketing
bars/restaurants/cafes

through traffic
through traffic

tour buses
public buses
taxis & private cars
to/from subway
(underground)
public buses
seabus
seabus
water taxis
tourist ferries
tourist ferries

02

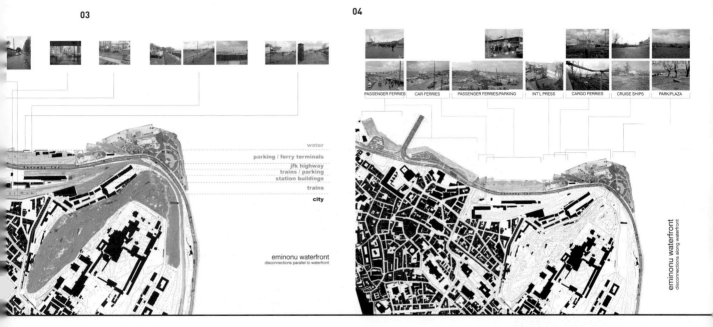

03

04

PASSENGER FERRIES   CAR FERRIES   PASSENGER FERRIES/PARKING   INT'L PRESS   CARGO FERRIES   CRUISE SHIPS   PARK/PLAZA

water
parking / ferry terminals
jfk highway
trains / parking
station buildings
trains
city

eminonu waterfront
disconnections parallel to waterfront

eminonu waterfront
disconnections along waterfront

02 PROGRAM DIAGRAM A direct underground connection is created between a new subway stop behind Sirkeci Station and the waterfront, where the passage opens to a series of terraced roofs with various uses. These occupiable roofs cover a series of more traditional cellular programs related to transportation, commerce, and entertainment.

03 DIAGRAM 1: EMINONU WATERFRONT The land between the city fabric of Eminönü and the Golden Horn is separated by infrastructure and architecture into distinct bands parallel to the water's edge.
04 DIAGRAM 2: EMINONU WATERFRONT The land along the waterfront in Eminönü is broken into distinct segments, each serving its own purpose and differentiated by its particular infrastructure and quality of open space.

05

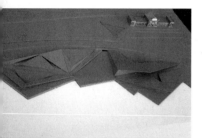

06

the city. Additionally, new programs can be inserted to promote social interaction between locals and tourists.

In terms of its physical manifestation, the project draws from existing infrastructural compositions found in Istanbul, especially the ways in which various modes of infrastructure connect with each other. First, the edge of the waterfront is changed from a straight line to a jagged edge. The jagged edge provides additional length to accommodate more ferries, while allowing the ferries to dock parallel to the water's edge (a necessity given the strong currents in the Golden Horn). Second, access roads are added to both sides of the Kennedy Highway. This allows for "through traffic" to continue unimpeded, while the access roads provide for pickup and drop-off zones at the ferry terminals to the north and Sirkeci Station to the south.

Between the "jagged edge" of the water and the "nudging edge" of the Kennedy Highway, the project incorporates an architectural language meant to unify the waterfront visually, as well as to maintain a sense of openness throughout. The roofs, which enclose commercial and transportation-related programs, are occupiable and continuous with the ground plane. The combination of program types (public open space on the roofs and in the central plaza; commercial shops, restaurants, and bars; and transportation-related stores) is meant to make the Sirkeci waterfront not only a pass-through zone for commuters but also a destination zone for locals and tourists, who may come to eat, drink, see a show, or just sit in the sun.

05 SITE PLAN The water's edge is reconfigured from straight to jagged to accommodate a higher number of ferries of multiple lengths, serving locals and tourists. Clearer connections are formed between the Kennedy Highway, the waterfront, and Sirkeci Station to accommodate pedestrian and vehicular transfers.

06 MODEL The new waterfront design is composed of folding planes that host different functions: ferry waiting, informal gathering, green space, and performance.

07

08

07 PHOTO MONTAGE Upon exiting the passage from the new underground subway station, passengers arrive at a plaza, flanked by commercial and entertainment shops, that opens up views across the Golden Horn toward Galata.

08 PHOTO MONTAGE The placement and slopes of the occupiable roofs create a variety of perspectives toward the city and across the Golden Horn. From the garden roof above the local ferry terminal, visitors gain a clear view to Topkapı Palace.

This project explores the formal and programmatic potentials of an urbanism based on a dense network of infrastructural systems. Sirkeci, located on the historic peninsula, is in a uniquely strategic location to take advantage of the potential 1.2 million passengers who will be using the Marmaray tunnel every day by the year 2015, given the proximate locations of both local and international transportation systems. Disregarding the city's vision of divesting Sirkeci of its current modes of transit, this proposal takes the position that a new urban-space typology can emerge from modal density and actually intensifies the existing system in response to, and in promotion of, a new understanding of the mobility of contemporary cosmopolites. This new type of public space, primarily based on transience, emerges from the connections between modes. It is a space in which the global and local are mutually inclusive and is supported through this proposal both formally and programmatically.

Formally, this proposal stems from the rational need for rapid intermodal connections—the lifeblood of any hub—and research into emerging connection methods. The territories of transportation and communication networks increasingly overlap. For example, a person taking a ferry across the Bosphorus can arrange via instant messaging for a car to be waiting when they get out of the subway station and for a water taxi to be available when they reach the water's edge. For this reason, the initial formal gesture is to create a large roundabout on Kennedy Highway, providing the fastest possible connection by car between the existing modes: car ferries, regional and international trains, tram, and pedestrian; the anticipated Marmaray tunnel station; and the proposed addition of an interregional bus station. Using the remote satellite terminal airport type as an organizational diagram, the various modes are arrayed as independent terminals along the roundabout, which provides both slow lanes for local connections, departures, and arrivals, and through-lanes for high-speed traffic, thus increasing the capacity for vehicles while solving the problem of congestion

01

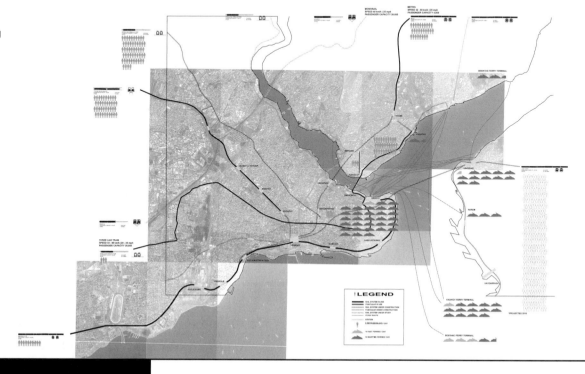

DAVID BROWN

01 SITE PLAN The project attempts to create a new urban-space typology emerging from an intensification of the existing system. A road loop is inserted to allow through traffic and connections between modes of transportation.

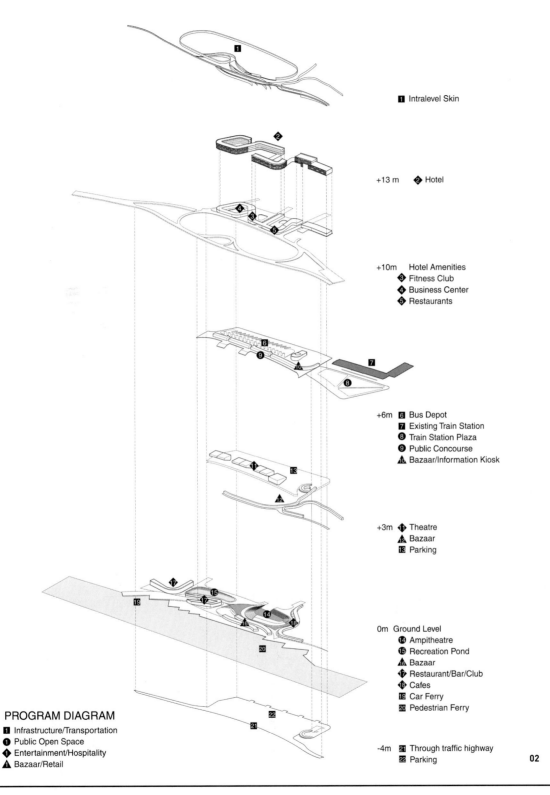

1 Intralevel Skin

+13 m   ◆ Hotel

+10m   Hotel Amenities
       ◆ Fitness Club
       ◆ Business Center
       ◆ Restaurants

+6m   6 Bus Depot
      7 Existing Train Station
      ● Train Station Plaza
      ● Public Concourse
      ▲ Bazaar/Information Kiosk

+3m   ◆ Theatre
      ▲ Bazaar
      13 Parking

0m Ground Level
       ◆ Ampitheatre
       ● Recreation Pond
       ▲ Bazaar
       ◆ Restaurant/Bar/Club
       ◆ Cafes
       19 Car Ferry
       20 Pedestrian Ferry

-4m   21 Through traffic highway
      22 Parking   02

PROGRAM DIAGRAM
■ Infrastructure/Transportation
● Public Open Space
◆ Entertainment/Hospitality
▲ Bazaar/Retail

along Kennedy Highway. The loop interior creates a large public plaza that provides pedestrian connections between the various modes. The road network is further articulated by being raised 6m above grade, allowing the edge of the plaza to be heavily programmed and providing connections to the surrounding areas.

The primary formal strategy of the public plaza is an excavation that provides visual and physical connections between the different modes and their associated programmatic needs—highways, parking, ticketing kiosks, and bus platforms. The form of the cellular program that lines the edge of the plaza creates an oscillating system of centrifugal and centripetal movement that causes the space to fold in and out of itself, preventing the proposal from becoming a closed system.

The programmatic strategy infuses the plaza with uses that fulfill the global and local aspirations of the proposal. The large plaza surface is differentiated into three loose zones programmed for various recreational uses. The excavation creates a large amphitheater in one area of the tripartite plaza that can be used for large festivals and outdoor cinema during the summer. The second major area contains a pond that is lined by a seating berm with views of the Golden Horn. The pond registers the temporality of the site through its seasonal uses, such as fishing in the summer and ice skating in the winter. Between these two areas is a small grove of trees in the middle of the plaza, which stretches into a landscape network that physically connects the three programmatic zones.

The edges of the plaza are heavily programmed with a bazaar, cafes, bars, nightclubs, and a cinema housed in the bus depot lining the southern edge of the plaza. In a curious reversal of the traditional nature of such programs, the bazaar is intended as a unique shopping experience for global tourists, whereas the nightclubs and cinema are provided as modern entertainment venues for locals. These programs also encourage twenty-four-hour activity in Sirkeci. Above the bus depot, a deck creates a virtual ground plane that houses a large hotel and business center and additional restaurants with amazing vistas of the Bosphorus and Golden Horn. The deck also provides historically absent connections from the existing city fabric to the Golden Horn water's edge, the new public space, and Kennedy Highway.

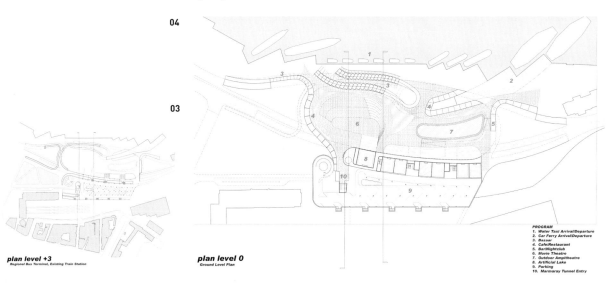

04

03

PROGRAM
1. Water Taxi Arrival/Departure
2. Car Ferry Arrival/Departure
3. Bazaar
4. Cafe/Restaurant
5. Bar/Nightclub
6. Movie Theatre
7. Outdoor Ampitheatre
8. Artificial Lake
9. Parking
10. Marmaray Tunnel Entry

plan level +3
Regional Bus Terminal, Existing Train Station

plan level 0
Ground Level Plan

03 PLANS A regional bus terminal, taxi drop-off, and parking offer additional transportation options at the site.

04 GROUND PLAN Cellular programs—such as a bazaar, restaurants, and bars—occupy the space directly beneath the

road loop. A movie theater, outdoor amphitheater, and informal open spaces fill the area within the loop.

05 SECTION PERSPECTIVES Along with the adjacent transportation functions, the area beneath the highway loop occupies commercial and nightlife businesses that activate the space at all times.

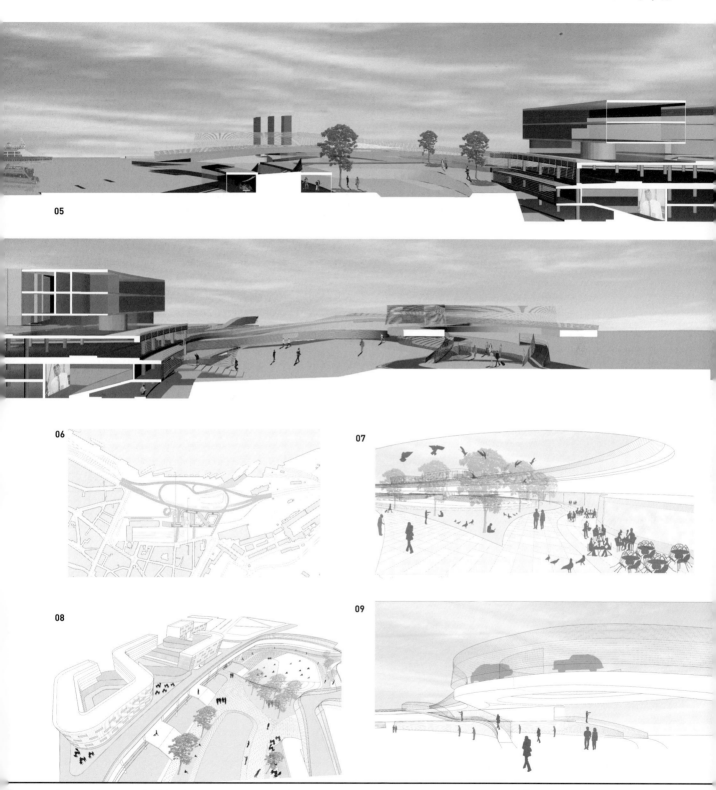

06 TRANSPORTATION DIAGRAM The large number of passengers who pass through Sirkeci every day by train, car, and ferry, and the number expected to use the new Marmaray Tunnel, necessitate a dense network of infrastructural systems at the site.

07 PERSPECTIVE VIEW Commercial and nightlife programs exist beneath the roadway, which is screened from the central space to reduce noise pollution.

08 AERIAL PERSPECTIVE A regional bus terminal, with hotels above, and a central public open space surrounded by commercial and nightlife programs create a setting where global and local visitors converge.
09 PERSPECTIVE VIEW The roadway is screened from the public spaces below to reduce noise and air pollution.

Examining the waterfront development in Istanbul, one sees that it is impossible to walk from the inner city to the waterfront. In the old Eminönü district, access is blocked by two arteries along the waterfront: Kennedy Highway and the train route. In this project, I proposed three main strategies to reconnect and revive the waterfront in the Sirkeci site. Also, I try to position these strategies in an urban design realm to find hidden potential in the physical urban space.

Linkage: Two main regional linkages occur in the Eminönü district. One is from the old city fabric to the waterfront, which affects local and tourist circulation. Another is the greenbelt along the waterfront, which functions as a linear park for various activities. Implantation: To implant a new greenbelt instead of the block artery, the train route was removed. The replacement is a light tram system with more stops along the route. Also, this tram route becomes a loop in the Sirkeci site, serving as a connector of different functions such as commercial, tourist, and commuting, and different physical spaces from old city fabric to the waterfront.

Reidentification: As a gate in the historic Istanbul area, the façade of the Sirkeci Station and the original light tram route next to the station are kept. However, people would gain a new orientation while entering the Sirkeci *meydan* from the underground tunnel.

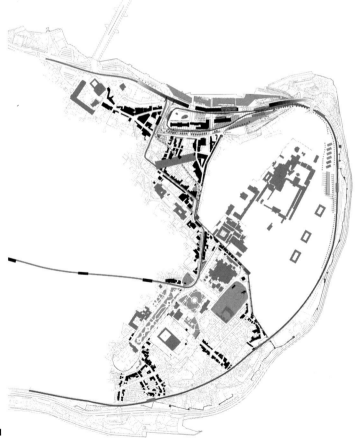

01

01 CONCEPT: HISTORIC SITES A continuation of the existing connections between historic sites and the Sirkeci waterfront site.

Implantation

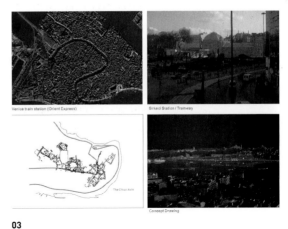

Re-identification

02

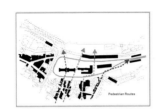

03

04

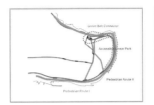
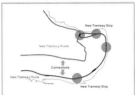

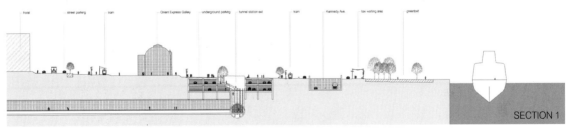

SECTION 1

SECTION 2

05

SECTION 3

02 STRATEGY: IMPLANTATION The implantation of the greenbelt is made possible by replacing the commuter rail with a light-rail loop.
03 STRATEGY: REIDENTIFICATION Perception and experience of the traditional buildings at Sirkeci will change with the new, underground approach from the subway.

04 LINKAGE Linkages are achieved on a local level through extension of the Sirkeci Street grid toward the waterfront, and on a city level through a reorganization of the tram service

05 TRANSVERSE SECTIONS The nature of the ground plane on the site is made lighter and more accessible by moving the Kennedy Highway underground, which opens up the ground level for green space and the light tram.

The objective of this project is to create an urban void within a dense area to serve as a plaza, and another void within this plaza for activities underground.

The orders seen in Istanbul vary, especially in terms of courtyard size and the way that the composition of the Topkapı Palace near the site has influenced the urban fabric. The project explores how service and servant spaces could be composed vertically, whereas these were arranged horizontally in the palace.

In 2007, both European and Asian continents will be connected by a tunnel under the Bosphorus, increasing the number of people arriving at this site. I have focused on current vehicular traffic, addressing the lack of adequate parking by creating a totally new concept in underground parking that frees the surface for human activities.

The parking area accommodates approximately 2,000 cars and enables users to experience an atmosphere difficult to create at ground level. There are also three major underground access tubes for pedestrians. The parking areas located in three underground floors are designed in nonlinear ways, which will create buffer spaces for people to interact. By aligning some of these spaces geometrically, it will allow trees to be planted so that people can experience nature vertically, and also ventilate the air inside. In the evening, car headlights flowing out from the voids will indicate activities underground. When there are enough activities, the lights will start to appear as one.

The site already has the potential for people to experience a horizontal dynamic from the perspective of the Bosphorus, although not the vertical dynamic that the Sultan experienced from the palace in earlier times. On the plaza, there will be voids to connect the activities above ground with the underground level, together with an open-air archeological museum. The voids have random geometric shapes derived from the car circulation underground.

Examining the waterfront development in Istanbul, one sees that it is impossible to walk from the inner city to the waterfront. In the old Eminönü district, access is blocked by two arteries along the waterfront: Kennedy Highway and the train route. In this project, I proposed three main strategies to reconnect and revive the waterfront in the Sirkeci site. Also, I try to position these strategies in an urban design realm to find hidden potential in the physical urban space.

Linkage: Two main regional linkages occur in the Eminönü district. One is from the old city fabric to the waterfront, which affects local and tourist circulation. Another is the greenbelt along the waterfront, which functions as a linear park for various activities.
Implantation: To implant a new greenbelt instead of the block artery, the train route was removed. The replacement is a light tram system with more stops along the route. Also, this tram route becomes a loop in the Sirkeci site, serving as a connector of different functions such as commercial, tourist, and commuting, and different physical spaces from old city fabric to the waterfront.

Reidentification: As a gate in the historic Istanbul area, the façade of the Sirkeci Station and the original light tram route next to the station are kept. However, people would gain a new orientation while entering the Sirkeci *meydan* from the underground tunnel.

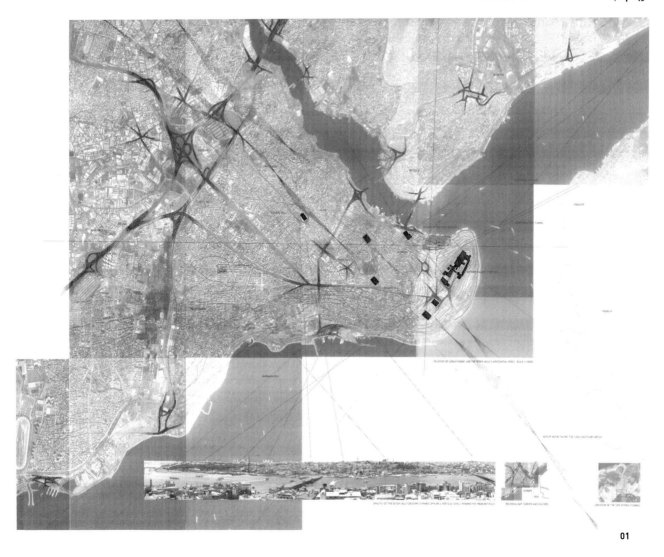

01

02

01 Relation between the urban fabric and the seven hills: analysis of the
seven hills creating Istanbul skyline
02 Perspective of activity in the underground and its relation to the ground level

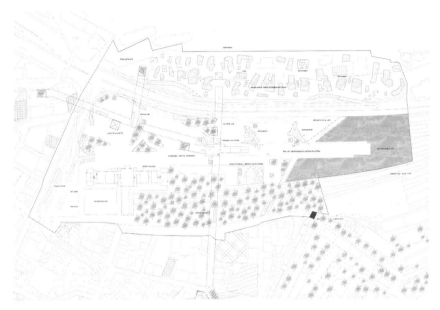

03

04

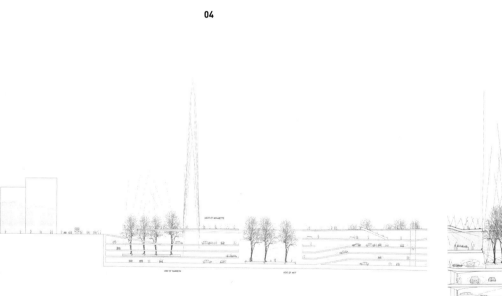

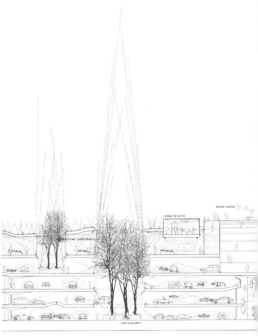

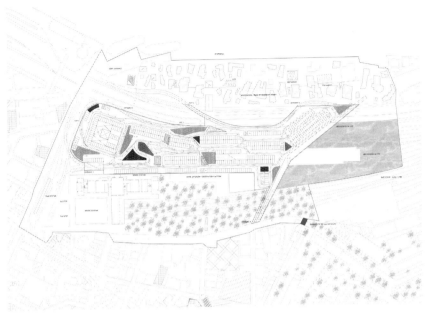

05

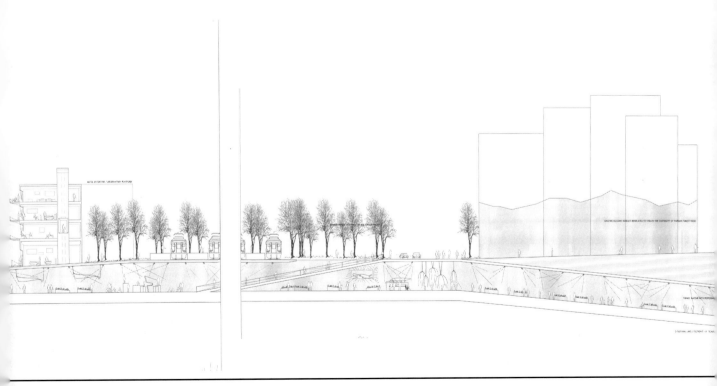

03 Ground floor plan with 1BF circulation
04 Section of the main vertical axis (the cultural line)
05 Basement plan with 2BF vehicle circulation

Istanbul's vision of Eminönü is one of segregation. The historic peninsula is to become primarily a tourist zone—a destination rather than a transit node. Sirkeci will be emptied of all transportation functionality, the train lines withdrawn to Yenikapı. Ferries will also be relocated to Yenikapı. It is not clear what will replace the train lines, but it is evident that the municipality views transportation as incompatible with other city amenities, such as recreation, tourism, and beauty. This attitude is also reflected in the proposed pedestrianization of several streets to the south of Sirkeci—cars are seen as unsuited to tourism. The municipality's adherence to segregation can also be seen in their intention to relocate industrial activity in Eminönü to the outer edges of the city.

I propose that transportation infrastructure can coexist with other urban functions. The strategic insertion of landscape and architecture will soften the edges between transportation and city, and then serve as new program—that is, the edges will become inhabitable as buildings and allées. Today, Eminönü is characterized by walls—walls that separate the trains from the city, Kennedy Highway from the waterfront, parking from the ferries. Landscape and architecture (trees and berms, buildings and ramps) will replace these walls, transforming obstacles into porous filters.

The instruments for this design proposal are primarily restoration ecology and landscape architecture. Three of the Sirkeci train lines will remain. Around them, in narrow bands, the other train lines will be replaced with trees that will remediate the soil (phytoremediation), which will allow the area to be safely occupied in ten to twenty years. Restoration ecology will also be the methodology for the waterfront: after passing through the three bands of trees in Sirkeci, the water will pass through one last filter—a thick line of trees on the northern side of Kennedy Highway. Once clean, the water will pass through either a constructed pool or runnels into the Golden Horn.

01

Buildings that are obsolete (such as small storage sheds) will be demolished and replaced with intimate-feeling "moments" within the long stripes, including along the waterfront. These will vary in size, height, and program: some will be sunken amphitheaters, others will be gardens, and still others will be restaurants or kiosks. This part of the design is also a strategic "insertion" of landscape in that it reuses existing infrastructure.

02

I believe this proposal could represent a formal strategy relevant to the urban design discipline as a whole: landscape as infrastructure. Living matter is (1) lubrication, which

03

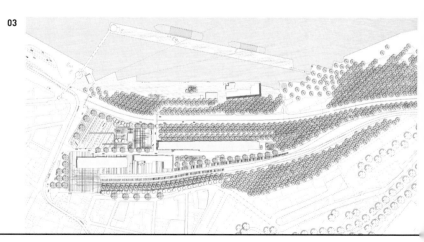

JUSTINE KWIATKOWSKI

01 PERSPECTIVE View looking from train tracks toward Sirkeci Station.
02 PERSPECTIVE View looking from Sirkeci Station along tracks.
03 SITE PLAN

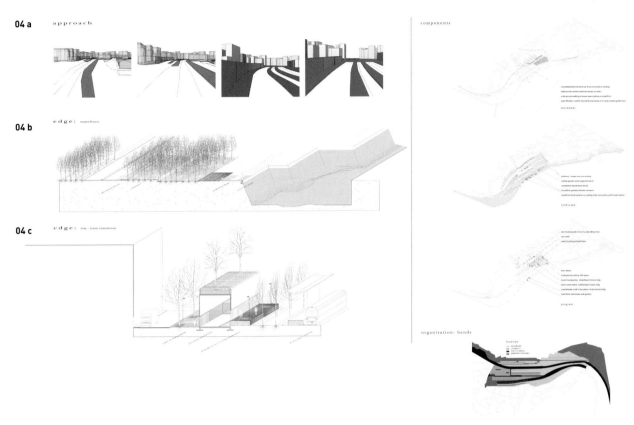

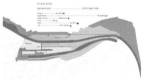

allows transportation infrastructure to move more easily through the city, (2) inhabitable space, which brings people into close but safe contact with transportation infrastructure, and (3) public works infrastructure, or technology that cleans water and soil. In other words, landscape creates public space while it makes intermodal transport more viable in central cities.

The design's formal manifestation of bands also reflects consideration for the skyline panorama of Istanbul; seen from Galata, the bands layer up in the human eye, creating the visual effect of mass vegetation. In other words, landscape creates a new visual identity for an area of a city. The urban peninsula becomes an inhabited forest.

There is one last aspect of this proposal that may be relevant to the urban design discipline: reuse. Landscape allows for the evolution of a city over time, without the total overhaul of the city. This may not always be the appropriate strategy, but it is useful in many circumstances, as shown by such high-profile projects as the Hi-Line in Manhattan (train becomes pedestrian path) and Fresh Kills in Staten Island (landfill becomes public park). In Sirkeci, too, infrastructure of one kind becomes infrastructure of another: train lines become water filters, and building foundations become public spaces.

04a,b,c PERSPECTIVES Views of the approach toward Sirkeci Station, and of the insertion of architectural and landscape elements between the tracks and on the waterfront.
05 DIAGRAM The components of the project include landscape elements integrated with new programs, as well as new circulation patterns between the various transportation nodes.

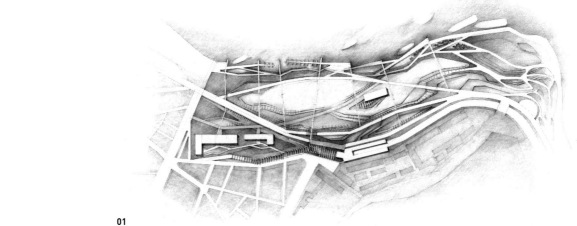

01

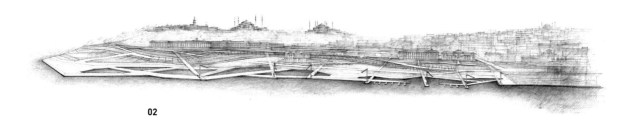

02

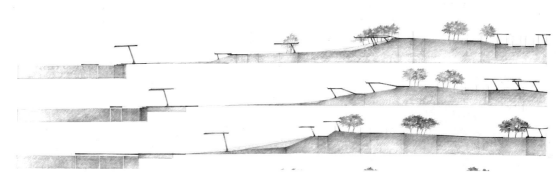

03

04

KOTCHAKORN VORAAKHOM

01 SITE PLAN
02 PANORAMA
03 TRANSVERSE SECTIONS A new layer of continuous grounds follows the existing skyline structure of Istanbul and helps enhance the ground line, eliminating the middle ground of megastructures that currently destroy the historical perception of the city.
04 SECTION PERSPECTIVE View looking east.

Multilayer urban design problems require complex solutions. As a landscape architecture student, I see no difference between the solutions offered by architecture, landscape architecture, or urban design because they are all related.

Landscape architecture, however, has more concern for the relationship of components, from human scale to that of the city. The openness component that landscape architecture provides act as a needed void in the dense city of Istanbul.

Throughout Istanbul's history, the city skyline has been a significant issue. The new continuous ground layer is part of the adjustment to the Istanbul skyline. The adjustment, which follows the existing skyline, helps enhance the ground line and eliminates the middle-ground megastructure, which destroys the historical perception of the city. The new ground, which reveals the city's history, is being treated as the landscape layer that subtly changes the face of Istanbul.

Using edge components in this big openness is what I aim to investigate in this design solution. To define the right edges is the key to successful functioning of the open space. Given the combination of transportation types and their different speeds, the diverse edges also act as small pockets of open space that help define this big open ground. The openness also provides flexibility for activities to spill out along the edge. The connectivity of city edge to landscape edge and to water edge creates both vivid and blurred boundaries to this open space.

From the point of view of program, this plan addresses the need for open space on a bigger scale than is provided anywhere else in town. This multipurpose open space will create liveliness in the city daily and also on special occasions.

The application of landscape elements that accommodate different-scale solutions and address issues of various edges, activities, and users is the main design solution. Answering an urban design problem using landscape elements lets the site's character answer its own question. Structures are created to reveal the site's topography and the potential for diverse uses. The static structure of edges and landscape elements provides the flexibility in use and offers a variable seasonal atmosphere to the city.

07

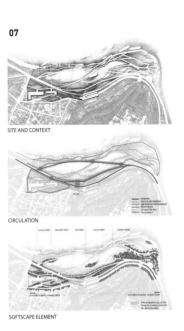

SITE AND CONTEXT

CIRCULATION

SOFTSCAPE ELEMENT

05 CONCEPTUAL MOVEMENT DIAGRAM

PROGRAM RELATED TO EDGE CONDITION

SPATIAL FUNCTIONAL DIAGRAM

PROGRAM

06 CONCEPTUAL LAYERS

CITY-WATER EDGE

TRANSPORTATION

LANDSCAPE

ACTIVITY

05 SPATIAL-FUNCTIONAL DIAGRAM
06 PROGRAM DIAGRAM Within the layers of landscape, transportation, and program, activities of varying scale can occur throughout the year.

07 SITE PLAN Primary circulation routes and softscape elements.

Istanbul is a city with much historic value. It is hard to appreciate this value, however, when so much of the historic district is void of cultural activities. The objective of the design for the new Sirkeci Station is to connect the various modes of transportation to alleviate congestion and give new life to culture.

The approach to the new design for Sirkeci Station was initially addressed by creating a series of strips or striations. These striations were then manipulated, creating a series of overlapping strips where multiple events could happen simultaneously. This concept addresses the multiple modes of transportation as well as the multiple users that are to inhabit the space.

The overlap occurs at various locations. First the trains (both local and international) slide underneath a new food court and pedestrian bridge that leads people to and from the interior fabric of the city and a new parking garage. This move also brings the tourist (international trains) to the historic Sirkeci Station, which will again act as a full-function station, the gateway between Europe and Asia. The biggest move made through design is a bridge for pedestrians and bicycles, which provides a greater connection out to the water and along the coastline. The bridge creates a space of leisure for citizens of Eminönü. This bridge that bifurcates and then molds back together overlaps both Kennedy Highway and the car-ferry entrance. Therefore cars and pedestrians can coexist in a safer condition. The bridge also leads tourists from Sirkeci Station to a new tourist center that helps visitors get around the city and connect to the ferries. The building's structure simply folds from the bridge, as does the new commuter station. The formal language is consistent, but houses different programmatic elements. The bridge is the spine that supports the various programmatic elements.

By bringing multiple programmatic elements for numerous inhabitants, new cultural events can take place along the Eminönü peninsula. The historic value of the city will never diminish, but with upgrades in transportation and a revival of the waterfront, the quality of life of the people of Istanbul will improve, along with the city's attractiveness to visitors.

01

02

03
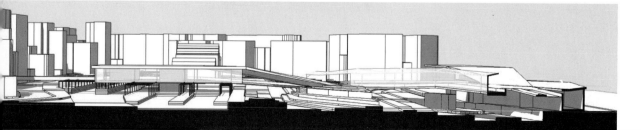

KRISTIN HOPKINS

01 MODEL Aerial view.
02 MODEL A connection is made between the Marmaray subway station and the pedestrian bridge crossing the Kennedy Highway.

03 TRANSVERSE SECTION Local and international trains slide underneath a new food court and pedestrian bridge that leads people to and from the interior fabric of the city. A pedestrian bridge then creates space of leisure for citizens, bifurcates and then molds back together, overlapping both the Kennedy Highway and the car-ferry entrance.

04

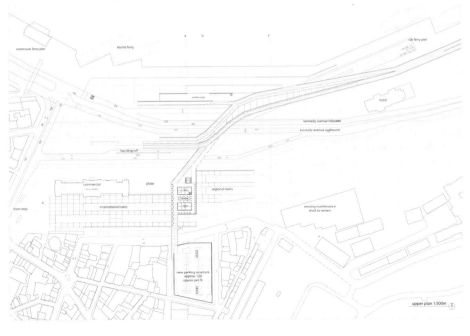

05

06

Striation Strategy
manipulation

intervention

positive

negative

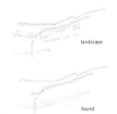

landscape

found

04 MODEL View looking west.
05 PLAN

06 CONCEPT: STRIATION A series of striations are
inserted as overlapping strips where multiple events can
happen simultaneously. This addresses the multiple modes
of transportation as well as the multiple users who will
inhabit the space.

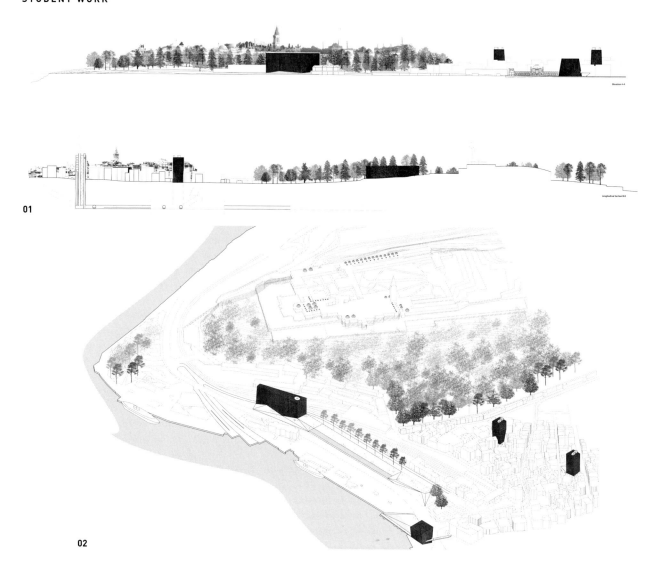

01

02

We are looking at a historic city, characterized by many layers of urban change over 2,000 years. How do you deal with both the heterogeneous character of the city and the difficulty of expropriating land in Turkey?

Instead of working on tabula rasa, I identified strategic points, or "wounds" in the city, that occur by the introduction of new transportation modes. In this case, we have the introduction of the Marmaray tunnel that will create clearings on the site and in the urban fabric of Istanbul.

Marmaray Tunnel (01 /02) Clearing of two urban blocks: The tunnel will clear two blocks within the urban fabric for ventilation shafts, emergency exits, and lift exit.

Trains (03) Clearing of Sirkeci Station hall; (04) Clearing of rail yards adjacent to highway: Sirkeci Station will be reduced to three international rail lines. Sirkeci becomes an international destination and a local hub. The regional hub is in Yenikapı.

NATALIE RINNE

01 SITE SECTIONS
02 AXONOMETRIC VIEW The interventions share a formal language that connects them, allowing people to measure themselves against the indeterminacy of the surroundings.

03 DIAGRAM: INTERVENTIONS Landscape transformations within the existing clearings will have an impact beyond the architectural interventions.
04 DIAGRAM: CLEARINGS Within the densely packed peninsula of Istanbul, clearings exist around significant public buildings.

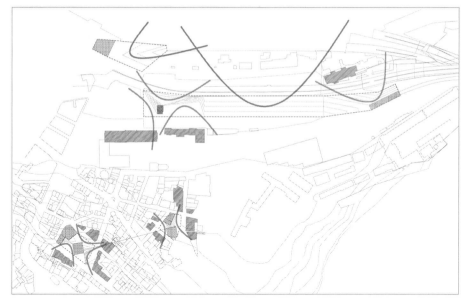

03

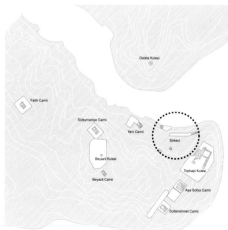

04

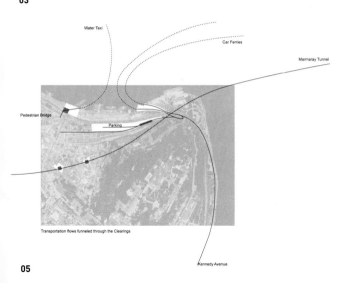

05

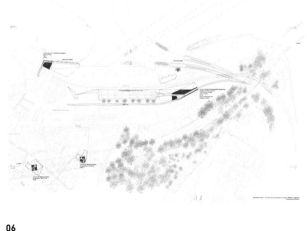

06

Ferries (05) Clearing of freight ferry terminal: The Marmaray tunnel trains will carry freight during the night. Ferries carrying freight will be eliminated in Eminönü.

Cars (06) Clearing of the car ferry terminal: Car ferries will keep their full capacity, because the Marmaray tunnel is exclusively operated for passenger trains and freight transport. The car terminal will, however, be relocated at the former freight ferry terminal, as it is more easily accessible from the highway, and relocation will reduce congestion at the highway exit to the historic district of Eminönü.

05 POINTS OF INTERVENTION Relationship between the project's interventions and the existing transportation network.

06 SITE PLAN Architectural nodes are linked to technical buildings servicing the transportation hubs. These nodes are starting points for public activity in the clearings that exist in the urban fabric.

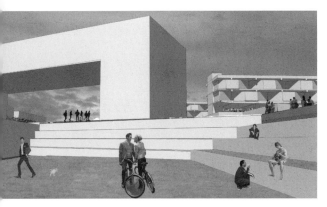

01

02

The site around Sirkeci Station contains multiple layers of information about built form that spans centuries. Its development offers challenges: the site is used by masses of commuters; it contains tracks from a now-underutilized nineteenth- century train system; it has an archeological area that cannot be built on; Topkapı Palace and the old city walls are in the southeast part of the site, and Kennedy Highway, built in the 1950s, crosses the northern part. Added to that will be the new subway tunnel project, which will require a station in the site. All these factors contribute to a location very difficult to address from a purist or "tabula rasa" approach. This intervention therefore uses existing buildings, infrastructural elements, and archeological and historic areas as a driving force for design and enhanced urbanity.

The first intervention will affect the rail tracks. By relocating the station to an existing military building, the site becomes open for public use. Then, by excavating the archeological site, this section can become a public amenity—an archeological park. By then placing the subway tunnel station in the middle of the site, this feature can become the new center for the project, permitting the growth of the utilized fabric toward the eastern tip. The buildings that served the rail system and Sirkeci Station will be reconverted to retail areas, and the old service station will be turned into an archeological museum.

The northern part of the project will contain buildings that will hold different programs in a vertical manner. The ground level will hold retail and roofed public areas; these activities can spill over into the spaces in between the buildings. The second level will vary from each building, some holding semipublic terraces overlooking the Bosphorus and others providing connector bridges above Kennedy Highway. The upper levels will contain office space, and below these buildings an underground spine will provide parking for the site.

03

04

05

OSCAR OLIVER

01 PERSPECTIVE OF ARCHEOLOGICAL PARK
02 PERSPECTIVE OF PEDESTRIAN BRIDGE ACROSS KENNEDY HIGHWAY
03 SECTION PERSPECTIVE Parking is provided beneath new developments containing retail and public space on the ground, and office space above.

04 AERIAL PERSPECTIVE LOOKING WEST The former train service building becomes the center of a new archeological park.
05 AERIAL PERSPECTIVE LOOKING EAST The street grid of Sirkeci is allowed to extend through the site by pulling the commuter train lines back toward the east.

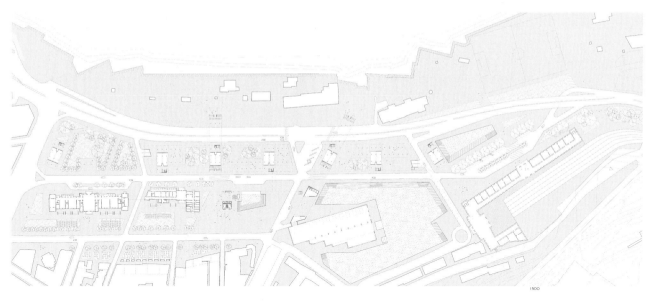

06

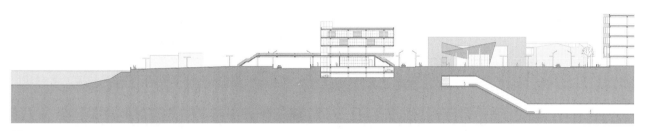

07

08

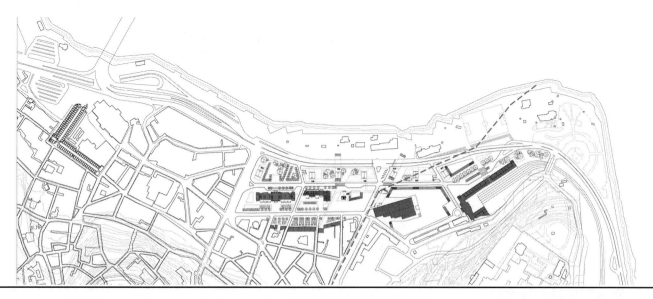

06 SITE PLAN Stopping the commuter rail lines further toward the east and converting the military building to a new train station allows for the extension of the Sirkeci street grid toward the Kennedy highway.
07 TRANSVERSE SECTION Pedestrian bridges allow for connections from the subway station across Kennedy Highway to the waterfront.

08 STRATEGY: BUILDING CONVERSION From east to west, the military building converts to a relocated train station, the train service building converts to an archeological site and museum, and the Sirkeci Station buildings convert to retail and museum spaces.

01

02

One of our first tasks this semester, while sifting through the piles of studio material, was to decipher a complicated (and in Turkish) map of Istanbul's transportation system. The lines of existing, under construction, and proposed forms of transportation gave the map the appearance of a dense network. While searching the internet for a map that showed just the existing transportation, I came across a diagrammatic metro map showing a series of parallel lines. The two maps seem to represent the two sometimes seemingly opposing aims of an effective transportation map—a multiplicity of nodes that allows the system to efficiently and comprehensively take you anywhere you want to go, and a system that is legible enough for you to figure out how to navigate it. A comparison of the maps of transportation systems around the world revealed that the number of lines is kept to a minimum while the number of nodes is intensified. This provides both legibility and the perception of efficiency.

The intervention attempts to intensify the number and directness of the connections between the existing modes of transportation on the site. While each form of transportation is distinctly legible, the concourse above connects them in myriad ways. The construction of the proposal is at the scale of infrastructure, serving as a catalyst for the textured human-scale development along and below it. The view corridors through the connecting elements provide another level of visual legibility just as the texture of the inhabitation would vary along the more commuter- or tourist-oriented paths, each detail infusing the network with the character of a node.

03

PHOEBE SCHENKER

01 PERSPECTIVE Pedestrian passageway between Sirkeci Station and the waterfront.
02 PERSPECTIVE Formally and informally programmed spaces within the new pedestrian connections between the various transportation nodes.

03 PERSPECTIVE Public open space between the new passageways.

04

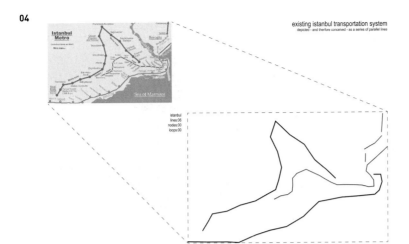

existing istanbul transportation system
depicted - and therfore conceived - as a series of parallel lines

istanbul
lines:06
nodes:00
loops:00

05

proposed istanbul transportation system
an increase in nodes - as well as the visual strengthening of exisitng
possible connection - converts the system into one which appears to
contain the possibility of arriving at any point in the city.

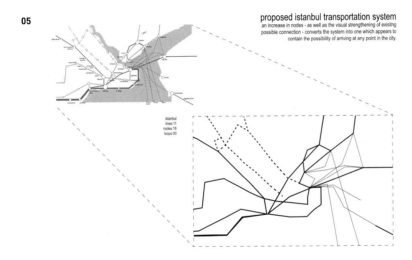

istanbul
lines:11
nodes:18
loops:00

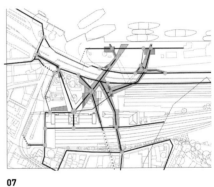

07

06

existing site pedestrian connections
a series of parallel sidewalks often lead to dead ends. many road
crossings are undefined, and pedestrians cut through parking lots, gas
stations, service yards.

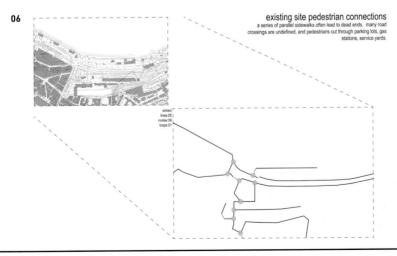

sirked
lines:05 |
nodes:09
loops:01

08

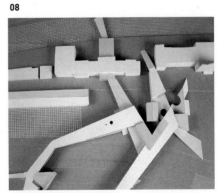

04 DIAGRAM Existing Istanbul transportation system depicted as a series of parallel lines.
05 DIAGRAM Proposed Istanbul transportation system, where an increase in
nodes and the visual strengthening of connections converts the system into one
that appears to offer the possibility of arriving at any point in the city.

06 DIAGRAM Existing pedestrian connections, in which parallel sidewalks often
lead to dead ends. Many crossings are undefined, forcing pedestrians to pass
through parking lots, gas stations, and service yards.
07 DIAGRAM Proposed intervention with pedestrian connections: By intensifying
the number of pedestrian connections, the proposal makes the system more effi-
cient; by varying the character of each connection, the paths remain legible.
08 MODEL Aerial view.

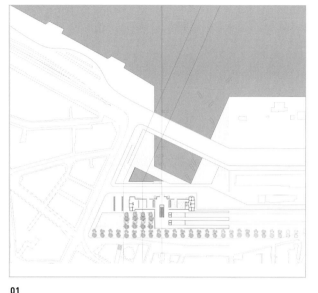

01

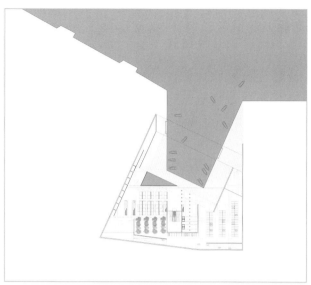

02

03

Istanbul's dense building fabric is made up of pieces from a broad range of historical periods. But unlike a sedimentary accumulation, where the oldest material makes up the lowest stratum, very old monuments punctuate the skyline in the old city of Istanbul. Our site is on the shoreline. A new tunnel connecting the Asian and European sides of the city is currently under construction and will have an exit on our site in Sirkeci Square. This tunnel exit completes the inversion of the sedimentary model—ancient monuments make up the skyline, and modern transportation emerges from below ground to create a monument on the shoreline.

Sirkeci Square is the historic European terminus for the Orient Express, and it is literally and conceptually on the fringe. In historic panoramic images, it is either outside the city wall, a void in the scene, or a place devoted entirely to transportation. It is a gap between the city fabric and the Golden Horn.

This shoreline monument to transportation is a hub for regional trains (which will continue to come into the old Sirkeci Station), the subway tunnel, water taxis, taxicabs, and a tram. The project also includes parking and retail. The new tunnel will reduce the need for ferry service crossing the Bosphorus, but will increase demand for local water-taxi service. By bringing water taxis in toward the old train station, the highly stratified transportation zone is crossed and the city fabric is connected to the water. The upper level of the transit hub is at the level of the old train station and the city. It includes the train station and taxi stand. Below the train station is the subway tunnel exit and water-taxi platform. Connections between the city level and the new water level are made through cuts in the ground plane, some of which contain stairs and escalators to facilitate movement between the layers of program. The lower-level plaza is a new *meydan*, most of which is occupied by water.

SARAH HOLTON

01 SITE PLAN Connections between the city level and the new water level are made through cuts in the ground plane. The lower level plaza is a new *meydan*, most of which is occupied by water.
02 PLAN The water's edge is cut to bring the Golden Horn closer to the city fabric.

03 PHOTO MONTAGE Aerial view of the project, looking east.
04 TRANSVERSE SECTIONS By bringing water taxis in toward the old train station, the highly stratified transportation zone is crossed and the city fabric is connected to the water.

04

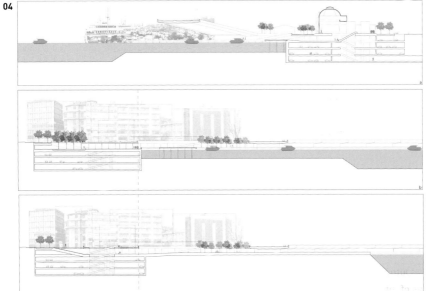

05

06

07

08

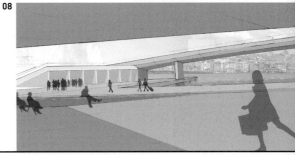

05 DIAGRAM: PANORAMAS A comparison of how the panorama of Istanbul has been viewed through history.
06 CONCEPT: INVERSION Whereas historical artifacts are usually buried beneath new constructions, Istanbul is a city where monuments rise above submerged, or subverted, modern transportation systems.

07 PERSPECTIVE View looking at ramps down to water-taxi level.
08 PERSPECTIVE View from escalators emerging from tunnel, looking under Kennedy Highway toward Galata.

A city with unmatched layers of political and architectural histories, Istanbul struggles to adapt its historical urban fabric and infrastructure to the contemporary demands of a modern society. Perhaps the most visibly challenged amenity—the transit network—is, in recent years, battling exponential population growth rates, an ever-expanding urban fringe, and a fragile historic core still functioning as a significant commercial and touristic hub for the city.

Over the past several decades, improvements have been made to link the historic peninsula with the districts fronting the opposite sides of the Golden Horn and the Bosphorus. Beginning with ferry transport, Istanbul has since implemented heavy passenger-rail lines, automobile bridges, and light rail lines in efforts to move people in and out of the historic core. Now the city has invested its efforts and money in a subway tunnel, dubbed the "Marmaray Project," which will provide the first train access between the Asian and European continents, beneath the Bosphorus and the historic peninsula.

The city plans to provide a single major transit hub at Yenikapı, a district near the outer southwest edge of the historic core, hoping to establish this location as the primary means of intermodal transit connections for the city. Meanwhile, they ignore the historic ethos and practical location on the northeast side of the peninsula, having little vision for the future of Sirkeci and dismissing it as just a minor part of the new Yenikapi-driven transit network.

This project proposal recognizes the inherent problems with funneling a large majority of multimodal transit users through a singular transit node, and instead suggests that perhaps the transit system should operate under a more diversified strategy of providing multiple transit options so that the historic urban fabric not be overburdened with a modern transit system that may soon again reach its carrying capacity.

Therefore this project proposes that the Sirkeci waterfront site be reconsidered as a major player in the Istanbul transit network. The historic site presents a fantastic opportunity to bring varying modes of transit together in a historic setting for the greater advancement of the city and its people.

At its foundation, this project explores the mat-building typology as it relates to intermodal transit activity. Many of the earlier historical precedents of this horizontal, layered typology contain varieties of uses, from Peter and Alison Smithson's housing schemes to

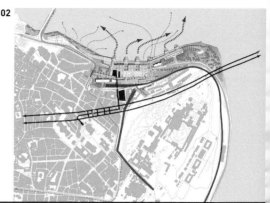

THOMAS HUSSEY

01 SITE PLAN The project aims to set itself apart as a new, modern structure, while working together with the existing transportation networks to create a hub of connections and programs that complement transit activity.

02 TRANSPORTATION NETWORK The project allows for the filtering of passengers between the different modes of transportation crossing through the site.

Le Corbusier's Venice Hospital. Perhaps the most successful (and replicated) use of the mat typology, however, is embedded in transit design throughout the world—a functional solution to dealing with intermodal transit connections while allowing for flexibility and future expansion. Norman Foster's Stanstead Airport and FOA's Yokohama Ferry Terminal, for example, clearly articulate the horizontal layers of use and critical vertical connections, direct and implied, between these layers.

This Sirkeci project strives to build on this relatively simple assembly of layering to apply an order of logic to the eight or so modes of transit entering and exiting the Sirkeci Square area. With a gradual change in grade between street level and water level, and with the addition of an underground train tunnel, the site inherently presents opportunities to negotiate level changes between modes of transit, and provides exciting opportunities to study the means of connection between these various levels.

03

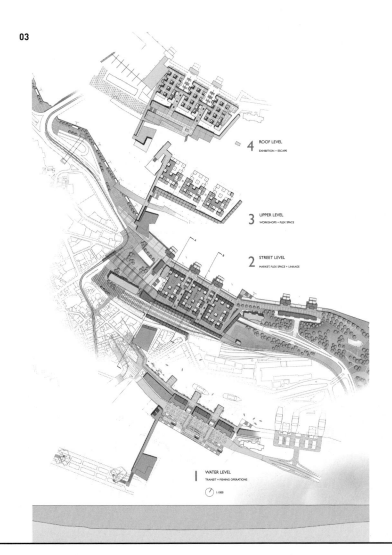

4 ROOF LEVEL
EXHIBITION + ESCAPE

3 UPPER LEVEL
WORKSHOPS + FLEX SPACE

2 STREET LEVEL
MARKET, FLEX SPACE + LINKAGE

I WATER LEVEL
TRANSIT + FISHING OPERATIONS

04

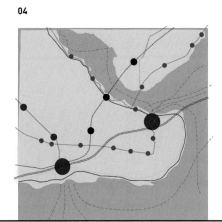

03 PROGRAM DIAGRAM
04 TRANSPORTATION DIAGRAM The project proposes that Sirkeci, along with Yenikapı, should be expanded into a major transportation hub to accommodate Istanbul's future needs.

Beyond transit, this project ultimately uses these transit connections and the resulting masses of users to introduce programmatic elements that complement the transit activity, respect the historical nature of the site and the peninsula, and allow for future changes in function.

Building on the history of the *meydan* as a flexible public space accommodating impromptu gatherings and markets, this contemporary mat strategy attempts to incorporate not only structured spaces (e.g., transit termini/stops, street market, fish market) but also flexible spaces to suit both recurring and sporadic events such as exhibitions and public performances, as well as landscaped plazas serving as platforms to view the historic panorama.

Programmatically the project takes on a highly contextual relationship, responding both to contemporary transportation needs and to historic activities of the site. Formally this mat structure also provides an ideal solution to working with the historic fabric of the city and unmatched skyline of the historic peninsula. Although jumping drastically in scale, to megastructure proportions, the project avoids any attempt to emulate or expand the ancient fabric of the city. By tying into the fabric only at key points of circulation, the project clearly sets itself apart as a contemporary building serving contemporary functions, not for the sake of self-image or pretension, but to preserve and showcase the precious character of the surroundings. Furthermore, while the horizontal scale of the project is immense, the vertical nature of the mat structure remains minimal. The result is an unadulterated skyline, a modern project harmonizing with the older buildings beyond and across the Golden Horn.

Ultimately, at the academic level, this project presents a strong argument for the mat building's role in architecture, or more important, urban design. Aside from the renewed and complex architectural testing of transit capacity within the mat structure, the most important aspects of this project relate more to the urbanism in which it is set and which in turn it produces. While many older precedents of mat building operate largely autonomously and internally, this project strives to rely on the urban context to solidify its role in its surroundings. With pedestrian streets seamlessly flowing in and out of the project, among the various types of program and transit connections, the project acts as an extension of the urban life outside its boundaries. This notion of layered uses and paths with ill-defined boundaries (both social and physical) leads to the term mat urbanism rather than mat building, as the project takes on a much grander role in the urban landscape.

05

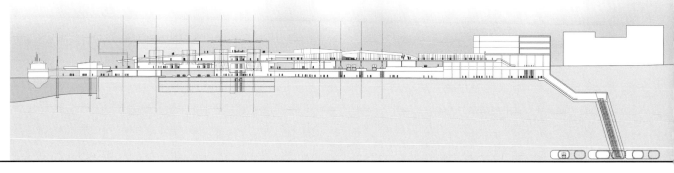

05 SECTION A The project extends to the new subway, while still allowing transportation to pass through in the opposite direction.
06 SECTION AXO Revealing the layers of program and vertical circulation within the mat building.

07 SECTION B Horizontal layers of activity are punctuated by critical vertical connections.

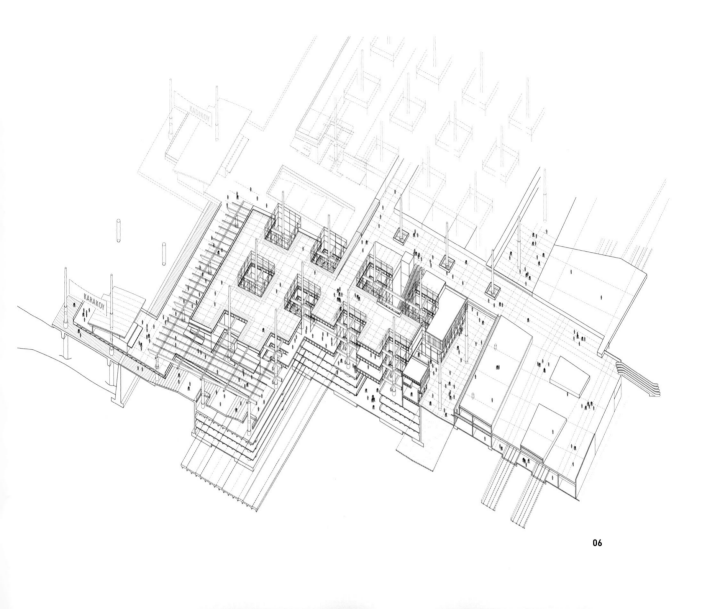

06

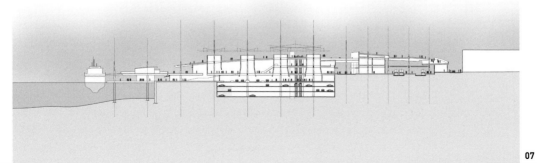

07

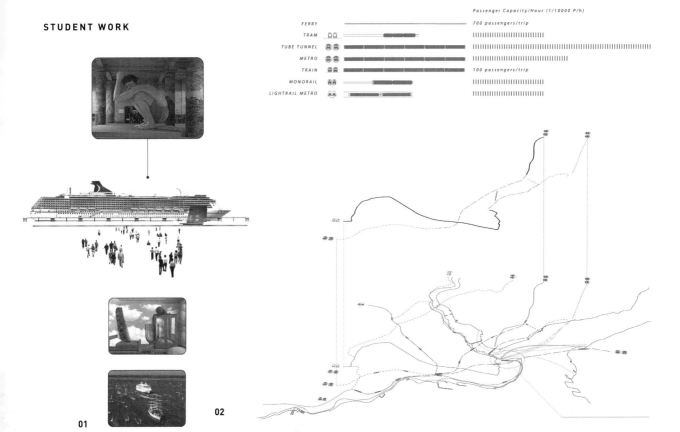

Passenger Capacity/Hour (1/10000 P/h)

FERRY		700 passengers/trip
TRAM		||||||||||||||||||||||||||
TUBE TUNNEL		|||||||||||||||||||||||||||||||||||||||||||||||
METRO		|||||||||||||||||||||||||||||||||||
TRAIN		100 passengers/trip
MONORAIL		|||||||||||||||||||||
LIGHTRAIL METRO		|||||||||||||||||||||

01

02

As Sirkeci is awaiting major transformations with the Marmaray subway tunnel project under way along with other large public transportation improvements around the area, this project provides a narrative for a new conception of program and site. The project deals with the reevaluation of the current conditions, problems, and potentialities, both spatial and economic, that will offer an alternate definition of the role of the place without breaking away from its traditional past.

This project has evolved under the speculation that the introduction of the new subway tunnel connecting the Asian and European sides of the city will reduce dependence on the use of the ferries to commute across the Bosphorus. The docks of Sirkeci, which served the British and French navies during the Crimean War and were later transformed to receive the ferries that commute to the Asian side of Istanbul, now await a new role.

The nineteenth-century gesture of extending the train lines around the peninsula up to Serkeci is reaffirmed through the introduction of yet another mode of regional transportation. The new 330-meter-long berth is capable of supporting the bigger cruise ships that do not find their place in outdated cruise-ship terminals around the city. The historic evolution of the site exposes a continuous dialogue between the landmarks and the waterfront. This is the most favorable point in the city to capture the image of the Orient that arriving Europeans want to see. Arriving almost at the level of the Topkapı Palace, the cruise ship introduces a new vantage point not only to the Square but to the city as a whole. The berth allows for smaller ship traffic to take place while the cruise ship is docked and doesn't disturb water activities that are beloved by Istanbulis.

AHMED KHADIER

01 CONCEPT IMAGES The project employs a scaling technique similar to that used in surrealist artworks, which causes the viewer to briefly confuse scales.

02 DETAIL PLAN Rerouting the highway opens up space to remodel the terrain and respond to infrastructural needs: terracing, lifting, spreading, and converging of various paths. The project is thus suspended between two scales: the grandiose gesture and the detailed articulation. The middle scale is intentionally dropped.

Kennedy Highway is pushed to the edge of the urban fabric to both occupy the grounds of the now-obsolete train tracks and to reconfigure the public spaces around it, creating a vast field adjacent to the waterfront. The repercussions of rerouting the road are tested in section and give way to the remodeling of the terrain to respond to infrastructural needs— terracing, lifting, or spreading, to allow for separation or merging of various paths. The project is thus suspended between two scales, the grandiose gesture and the detailed articulation. The middle scale is intentionally dropped. Curb lines are pulled in flush with the tarmac and are replaced by bollards to emphasize the condition of "field." The cuts in the ground plane become curbs that are blown out of scale. This is an extension of the fact that the cruise ship is deployed as a rescaling element, rendering everything next to it minute in scale. This is a scaling technique present in surrealist art, causing the viewer to confuse scales for a brief moment. An influx of population takes place on the site once the cruise ship arrives. The crowds are diffused to the various local transportation modes that the site already hosts, and the site is depopulated in a few hours, then awaits the next influx of crowds.

03

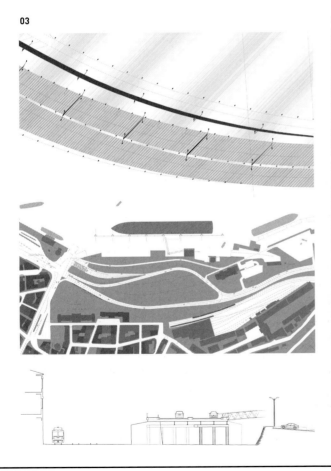

04

03 SECTION DETAIL The repercussions of rerouting the road are tested in section. Curb lines are pulled in flush with the tarmac and are replaced by bollards to emphasize the condition of "field." The cuts in the ground plane become curbs that are blown out of scale.

04 AERIAL PHOTO MONTAGE A large-scale cruise ship offset from the vast emptiness of the waterfront creates a new vantage point on Istanbul's landmarks and allows local ship traffic to continue operating between the cruise ship and the waterfront.

THE AGA KHAN PROGRAM FOR ISLAMIC ARCHITECTURE AT HARVARD AND MIT

Based at Harvard University and the Massachusetts Institute of Technology, the Aga Khan Program for Islamic Architecture (AKPIA) is dedicated to the study of Islamic art and architecture, urbanism, landscape design, and conservation, and the application of that knowledge to contemporary design projects.

The goals of the program are to improve the teaching of Islamic art and architecture, promote excellence in advanced research, enhance the understanding of Islamic architecture, urbanism, and visual culture in light of contemporary theoretical, historical, critical, and developmental issues, and increase the visibility of Islamic cultural heritage in the modern Muslim world. Established in 1979, AKPIA is supported by an endowment from His Highness the Aga Khan. AKPIA's faculty, students, and alumni have played a substantial role in advancing the practice, analysis, and understanding of Islamic architecture as a discipline and cultural force.

THE AGA KHAN PROGRAM AT THE HARVARD UNIVERSITY GRADUATE SCHOOL OF DESIGN

Established in 2003, the main aim of the Aga Khan Program at the GSD is to study the impact of development on the shaping of landscapes, cities, and regional territories in the Muslim world and to generate the means by which design at this scale could be improved.

The program focuses on the emerging phenomena that characterize these settings and on issues related to the design of public spaces and landscapes, environmental concerns, and land use and territorial settlement patterns. The process entails a study of their current conditions, their recent history (from World War II to the present), and, most important, the exploration of appropriate design approaches.

The program sponsors new courses, option studios, faculty research, workshops, conferences, student activities, and publications. It is supported by a generous grant from the Aga Khan Trust for Culture.

TITLES IN THE AGA KHAN PROGRAM BOOK SERIES

Two Squares, edited by Hashim Sarkis with Mark Dwyer and Pars Kibarer

A Turkish Triangle: Ankara, Istanbul, and Izmir at the Gates of Europe, edited by Hashim Sarkis

Han Tumertekin: Recent Work, edited by Hashim Sarkis